THE ARK FILE

THE ARK FILE

BY RENE NOORBERGEN

PACIFIC PRESS PUBLISHING ASSOCIATION
Mountain View, California
Omaha, Nebraska Calgary, Alberta

Books by Rene Noorbergen:

The Ark File
Charisma of the Spirit
Ellen G. White: Prophet of Destiny
You Are Psychic
Jeane Dixon: My Life and Prophecies

Library of Congress Catalog Card No. 74-79956

INTRODUCTION

In May, 1949, Radio Moscow broadcast a news item that focused world attention on the exploration plans of a small American group called the Oriental Archaeological Research Expedition. Claiming that their announced plans to explore Mount Ararat were nothing but a clumsy attempt to cover up Western espionage operations on Russia's border with Turkey, the broadcaster warned the expeditioners to stay away.

The warning penetrated millions of homes, but its effect proved exactly the opposite of what had been intended. Suddenly both vocal and financial support began to find their way into the home of Aaron J. Smith of Greensboro, North Carolina, leader of the group, and plans to locate Noah's ark on Mount Ararat in old Armenia received an electrifying jolt.

For several hundred years, rumors about the survival of the world's oldest ship had made the rounds of amateur archaeologists. Stories about a gigantic ship caught in the glaciers of the snow-covered mountain kept breaching the wall of Ottoman indifference, and the West listened, interested but wondering. The only basis for the claims was the Bible account of deluge, and that, to many, seemed just plain unbelievable.

Not until 1872 did the first meaningful piece of evidence supporting the Biblical flood surface. The evidence was inscribed in cuneiform among 20,000 clay tablets discovered in that year by George Smith, the British orientalist, among the ruins of a palace of the Assyrian King Ashurbanipal (669-626 B.C.). Startling was the fact that not only did the cuneiform inscriptions reveal names and events already known from the Bible, but they also brought to light a Babylonian version of the deluge now known as the Gilgamesh Epic.

It became a source of controversy among Bible students of various persuasions. "Where did the story originate?" they questioned. "Do both share a common cause, or did Moses borrow his deluge account from the Babylonians?" Whatever the cause—and we'll return to this later on in this book—there must have been a historical basis for the story. The discovery of the Babylonian deluge epic planted a seed that grew and grew.

Statistical studies and comparisons made in the privacy of scholars' laboratories are not always sufficient. Today's generation demands to be "in" on the discoveries. They want free access to undigested and uninterpreted facts so that they can relate them to their own experience. They not only want to see and hear, they want to feel, to be one with reality of history.

It remained for Dr. A. J. Smith, dean of the People's Bible School in Greensboro, North Carolina, to take up the challenge posed by the mysterious relationship between the Gilgamish Epic and the Biblical deluge account, and initiate the modern search for the most controversial artifact historians have ever recorded—Noah's ark.

Smith's Sacred History Research Expedition's probe on Mount Ararat in 1949 started a chain reaction of investigations all aimed at locating the remains of the ark. After comparing historical reports dating back thousands of years with more recent secular accounts mentioning the existence of a shiplike object on the slope of the 17,000-foot mountain, Dr. Smith became convinced that even though his expedition failed in its mission, the ark had to be there. Dr. Richard Andree, a German scholar, supported the concept of a worldwide flood wholeheartedly. In the course of his research, he compiled at least 88 different flood traditions gathered from nations and tribes around the world. Smith's devoted persistence has become the cause for the feverish Ararat activity which has continued since his 1949 expedition.

The later editor of a leading journal of exploration and discovery reportedly commented, "If the ark of Noah is ever discovered, it will be the greatest archaeological find in human history, and the greatest event since the resurrection of Christ. It will alter all the currents of scientific thought."

It is to all those who search for the ark that this book is dedicated.

Rene Noorbergen
Collegedale, Tennessee
January, 1974

CHAPTER 1

"In the six hundredth year of Noah's life, on the seventeenth day of the second month, on that very day the fountains of the great abyss were all broken open and the windows of heaven were opened. (The rain fell on the earth for forty days and nights.)"[1]

"And when the storm came to an end and the terrible waterspouts ceased, I opened the windows and the light smote upon my face; I looked at the sea, tentatively observing, all humanity had turned to mud, and like seaweed the corpses floated.

"I sat down and wept, and the tears fell upon my face."[2]

"On the seventeenth day of the seventh month the ark grounded on the mountains of Ararat."[3]

Four thousand four hundred years later, more or less, a Royal Dutch Airlines plane, flight KL 401, determinedly roared its way over the historical Bible lands of the Middle East—destination Amsterdam.

With a sigh of relief I had fastened my seatbelt and had cast one final look at the sweltering airport of Beirut. It had been quite a summer, but this was to be the last flight in a series of assignments that had again taken me around the world, and it felt good to be on the way home. A lengthy list of magazine assignments for Camera Press Limited of London had catapulted me into revolt-torn Laos to join youthful but ambitious Captain Kung Le and his ill-clad batallion of the Royal Lao Army on a Communist liquidating action in the Land of the Thousand Elephants. Then came Mussoorie, India, where I had a week's interview with the Dalai Lama, mentally reliving his dramatic escape from the invading Red Chinese. I visited other world hotspots, finally ending the trip with a sojourn to old familiar hangouts on the Gaza Strip.

But now the stories had been filed, and I was on the homestretch, ready for new adventures. Lugging a battered suitcase crammed with dirty shirts, and with a mind still drenched by a torrent of new and some not-so-new impressions, I had checked out of the Rabeiz Hotel in Ras-Beirut and dragged myself aboard the shiny DC-6, determined to sleep all the way home. Not a thing was going to keep me from it!

Somehow destiny had decided differently.

A pleasant yet disturbing sound kept interjecting a note of disharmony into my otherwise soothing dreams. Even jamming the pillow down around my ears didn't seem to help; it only caused the irritation to change into a mild chuckle, culminating in a ripple of suppressed laughter.

"Newspaper, sir? New York *Herald Tribune* perhaps?"

The cooing of the smartly dressed stewardess began to take effect. Drowsily I lowered my arm and with it went the second pillow, which I had acquired during my interrupted sleep. I squinted appreciatively at the "newspaper boy" who smilingly waited for my reaction.

I rubbed the sleep from my eyes.

"*Tribune?* Yes, I'll take one."

Scarcely awake, but now filled with good intentions, I wearily began to scan the pages, pulling my legs out of the aisle to make room for the passing cocktail wagon. Judging from the headlines, it seemed I really hadn't missed that much after being out of touch with the West these past few months. One of the ten-most-wanted fugitives had finally been apprehended by the FBI; President Eisenhower had made another of his well-meant political speeches; and Richard Nixon had once again captured a few columns by urging a renewed investigation of reputed subversive activities of the underground Communist Party, U.S.A.

It wasn't until I turned to an inside page that an eight-line news item caught my attention. An officer of the Turkish army, Captain Ilhan Durupinar, an Associated Press dispatch reported, had been examining aerial stereo photographs made during a routine reconnaissance flight over Eastern Turkey as part of a NATO project and had discovered what appeared to be a ship-like image on one of the negatives shot over the Ararat mountain range. The Turkish Army Cartography Department had turned the negatives over to Professor Arthur Brandenberger of Ohio State University for further study. The article ended by stating that Professor Brandenberger tended to agree with the first evaluation made in Turkey that the object might well be the remains of the legendary ark of Noah!

It was the best eight-line shot of adrenalin I had ever had! Noah's ark, indeed! Since my involvement in 1946 with the *Sacred History Research Expedition,* an organization created specifically to locate the ark, I had come to regard this as the most fascinating story I ever encountered. Much had happened since catching my first case of "ark fever," but now, with my magazine assignments safely in London, I became obsessed with the thought that this news story just might materialize into the realization of a newsman's dream.

Skeptical by nature, I had made a careful and diligent study of the various facts and legends which formed the basis for the diverse ark traditions and had arrived at the growing conviction that the underlying cause had to be a hard historical event; a story of a tragedy based upon facts, not mere hearsay.

Noah's ark! I remember gazing out the small window as the

plane roared onward. Floating high above the cottonlike bed of cumulus clouds, I began to formulate a careful plan of action. Even though Professor Brandenberger ranked high on the priority list of people to be contacted, ahead of him loomed the name of Dr. Aaron J. Smith, President of the People's Bible College in Greensboro, North Carolina, and executive director of the *Oriental Archaeological Research Expedition.* It was this organization which had initiated a search for the ark in 1949 but returned after a summer's work on the mountain, empty-handed but one experience wiser.

I had assisted Dr. Smith in organizing his expedition but had lost contact with him following the futile attempt of 1949. That was a decade before; yet once again the same story vied for headlines and began to haunt me.

My stay in Amsterdam was a short one; in London it was even shorter. Three hectic days later I found myself stepping down from a Greyhound bus at the Greensboro, North Carolina, bus terminal. A taxi dropped me off at the home of Dr. Smith.

It was a weak but conscious Aaron Smith who awaited me in his sickroom. He was no longer the same man I had known in the late 40's. Terminal abdominal cancer had transformed him from a stocky, dark-haired bundle of controlled energy into a skeletonlike caricature of his former self. With hollow eyes, translucent skin, and the tired pumping of his heart visible, he called me over to his bed.

"Is it the ark again, Brother Noorbergen?" he whispered. He always called me brother.

I nodded, clasping his hand in mine.

"Yes, Dr. Smith. I am here to tell you about some new Turkish aerial photographs which—"

"I have heard about them," he murmured, interrupting me, mustering all of his strength to show his enthusiasm. "Mother," he called. "Mother, Brother Noorbergen is going to find the ark. He's going to Turkey to find the ark."

He raised his trembling hand and pointed toward two four-drawer filing cabinets jammed against a corner of the adjacent storage room.

"There is everything you need to complete your research work," he whispered hurriedly, as though sensing his time was running out. "That's all I can leave you. Take it; combine it with your material; and together it'll be enough to pinpoint the location of the ark. Go, get it. It's all yours."

As Dr. Smith sank back onto his pillow, I turned and reached for the files, probing to find the missing links in this age-old mystery of world destruction.

Aided by the "Smith files," my renewed involvement in 1960 resulted in a search on the Ararat mountains as part of the Archaeological Research Foundation, an experience which in its own way created another enigma. But more concerning this in a later chapter. The following year, however, I dropped the ark project again—for another ten years. Magazine assignments, the writing of my first book, and family commitments all helped to push the ark deeper into the recesses of my mind. Yet always the "Smith files" rated an important place in my growing library. Not a year would pass but that I would leaf through them, dreamily recalling my previous journalistic entanglement with the possible whereabouts of the rescue vessel of the family of Noah.

Thus it remained for years until a wintry Sunday in February, 1970. Fairfax, Virginia, lay tucked in under a thick blanket of powdery snow. It had been a savagely cold night, but during the early morning hours a myriad of tiny snowflakes had captured the countryside and turned the morning into a crunchy, frosty fairyland. Flake after flake drifted lightly down to earth, fighting for survival as it fell. From my library window an occasional sled could already be seen swishing down the snowy slopes across the fields, and the bright red and green colors of waving stocking caps were set off by happy laughter as the children tasted the delightful freshness of the snow.

I grabbed for my overcoat. For several weeks now I had been planning to check on some books at the Potomac Book and Bible House in Takoma Park, a suburb on the other side of Washington. Even though this day seemed far from ideal for a twenty-mile ride, I decided to join the crowd and ignore the flood of snow-alert warnings. Plowing virgin tracks in the freshly fallen snow, I left the house and turned the wheels toward the Washington Beltway.

While I was leaving Mantua Hills, two other people departed from their homes bound for the same destination—Maria Hirschmann, a former member of Germany's Hitler Jugend, to autograph copies of her book *I Changed Gods,* and Ralph Crawford, a retired minister, to meet her at the store. Both were acting a part in a seemingly predestined plot.

To say that there is no vanity in authors would be a classical understatement, for when two of them meet, their published books and future projects are usually the first topics of discussion. It proved no different in this case.

Meeting Maria Hirschmann coincided with the time my book *Jeane Dixon—My Life and Prophecies* was celebrating its place on the 1969 national bestseller lists. Interest in Jeane's life and her psychic ability was at a peak. Within minutes after I met Maria, her bubbling enthusiasm suggested an exchange of books.

"Take mine with you," she offered, pressing an autographed copy in my hands. "I'll drop by your house on the way to the airport this afternoon and pick up yours."

Accompanied by an even more impressive sounding chorus of radio snow bulletins, I headed for home, cutting new tracks while pulling into my driveway. It was well past Maria's departure time from Dulles International Airport when the doorbell chimed. An elderly gentleman stood framed against the wintry sky.

"I am Ralph Crawford," he said and smiled apologetically. "I have come in Maria's place. She didn't have time to stop by on her way to Dulles and asked me to get a book for her and mail it."

With his abundant weight exceeding two hundred pounds, he made a grand impression. I invited him in and we settled comfortably on the family-room couch. The topic of conversation soon drifted to the various elements of writing that can skyrocket a book to fame or bury it forever.

"Speaking about that," he mused, "perhaps you can help me. I have with me a manuscript—a diary written by a Frenchman which deals with his reported discovery of Noah's ark. I have acquired the American rights and am trying to find a publisher for it."

Noah's ark? Someone had found Noah's ark? He doubtless interpreted my astonishment for a sign of pregnant interest, for he unhesitatingly continued, "I am president of Search Foundation, Inc., and our purpose is to clarify the mysterious whereabouts of the ark once and for all. Mr. Navarra, the Frenchman, is one of our people. Can I possibly interest you in helping us?"

I felt as if all blood drained from my face, and for a brief moment I must have looked more than just perplexed.

Crawford stopped.

"Did I say anything wrong?"

"You *did* say Noah's ark, didn't you?" I queried.

He nodded.

"Of all the stories I have ever investigated, this one is the most elusive," I said, speaking slowly, emphasizing every word. "I have been researching this ark mystery from the first moment I became involved with the Sacred History Research Expedition in 1947. Following that I was a member of the Oriental Archaeological Research Expedition, the A. J. Smith group. Then there was my connection with the 1960 expedition with George Vandeman, Dr. Siegfried Horn, and Wilber Bishop." But Ralph Crawford had already lost me. The look of surprise and bewilderment that had previously touched my face now covered his. Fingering his glasses nervously, he stared fixedly ahead.

"Can this possibly be the missing link I have sought after these past ten years?" he muttered more to himself than to me. "There is still so much we don't know; there are still so many facts and documents that I know have to be *somewhere.*" He paused, and we both stood silently lost in thought.

"Tell me," he continued. "Do you perhaps have any information on the old 1950 and 1960 expeditions? I have been able to account for every man of that last group except one, and he is supposed to have all of the original research material given him by the leader of the 1950 expedition. He used it for the Archaeological Research Foundation's 1960 expedition, but the others who were with him on Ararat will not disclose his name or any further clues as to his whereabouts. They seem to want to keep him under wraps until such time as they may need his material again. All I have been able to find out is his first name—Rene."

I couldn't conceal my glowing delight any longer.

"Mr. Crawford, your search is over! I am Rene. I am that man you've been looking for. I was the one who backed the 1960 expedition with the Smith material. The files are downstairs. They're yours if you need them. You've just reached the end of the trail."

Destiny? Luck? Providence? Some things are difficult to explain, especially when the various factors cannot be defined. This was certainly one of those moments when ordinary explanations failed.

For a while only the ticking sound of the proud old grandfather clock could be heard in the room. Both of us were involved with our own private thoughts. Then suddenly, as if moved by the same compelling force, we both stood up, and Ralph Crawford followed me down to the library where I reached for the fingerworn files of Dr. A. J. Smith.

One search had just ended; another search was about to begin.

The story concerning a God-fearing man and his family who escape in a wooden boat to avoid a watery death has always held an important place in both sacred history and mythology. To many people the question whether it was actually a chance escape or an event in which one man's family was lovingly prepared by a Higher Power and told to build a boat is really immaterial. It was the *event,* not the cause, that gave rise to the countless number of Deluge or Flood traditions treasured in the folklore and history of most tribes and nations, and it is this reported event that has stirred the imagination.

Research into the possible whereabouts of the ark has never really been coupled to the theological reasons for the Flood; instead it has centered on historical and legendary accounts. Up until the very moment that the modern search for the ark had its birth in southern California when H. M. S. Richards, Sr., Eryl Cummings, and Benjamin Allen were involved in forming the Sacred History Research Expedition in 1946, it was generally accepted that the Biblical account of the Flood was one of the oldest sacred narratives of the tragedy in existence. However, in two consecutive letters written by Dr. Phillip W. Gooch, another interested "ark-eologist," to Dr. A. J. Smith, a bombshell was dropped.

Quoting from what he claimed were ancient records reported to be in the possession of a Masonic order to which he belonged, Dr. Gooch relayed the following information to an unsuspecting Aaron Smith:

"There was a living witness on the ground who covered all the fine details of what went on during the Flood and after the Flood until her death in her 547th year," he wrote to Smith. "She was God's living witness, Noah's daughter-in-law, the wife of his son Japheth, a student of Methusaleh under whom she was apprenticed and who taught her all that had *preceded* the Flood. She was educated in all of the history of the human race up to that time. Her book—she called it her diary—is filled with things that occurred from Adam to her death and seems to me the most complete record of early human history ever recorded.

"Many of the problems confronting geologists today can easily be understood after one reads Amoela's Diary.

"At her death, dying in the arms of her youngest son, Javan, her diary was placed in her mummified hands in a crystal quartz case, with tempered gold hinges and clasps, and was discovered by a high-ranking Mason in the latter part of the last century. The original and the translation are now in possession of the Order.

"Our Commission investigated the manuscript, and all the history of the human race from Adam to her death was carefully catalogued. Everything that has been checked thus far has been proven to be true as far as we can determine." Although the correspondence between Drs. Gooch and Smith continued for years following that initial astonishing letter, nothing could coerce Gooch to reveal more information regarding Amoela's Diary or its whereabouts, even though in many of his letters he indicated a serious effort on his part to obtain an accurate translation for Dr. Smith. Nothing ever came of it. As promising as it seemed at the outset, the search that followed, checking museums and libraries, failed to produce any leads remotely supporting Dr. Gooch's claim.

Consequently, the oldest sacred account of the Flood in existence was still the Biblical story found in the book of Genesis. In chapters 6:9 through 8:22 we find the basis for all ark research; the standard against which all traditions and legends appertaining to this first recorded worldwide catastrophe should be measured.

The Bible records the tragedy. Taylor paraphrases it as follows, beginning with verse 12 of Genesis, chapter six:

"As God observed how bad it was, and saw that all mankind was vicious and depraved, he said to Noah, 'I have decided to destroy all mankind; for the earth is filled with crime because of man. Yes, I will destroy mankind from the earth. Make a boat from resinous wood, sealing it with tar; and construct decks and stalls throughout the ship. Make it 450 feet long, 75 feet wide, and 45 feet high. Construct a skylight all the way around the ship, eighteen inches below the roof; and make three decks inside the boat—a bottom, middle, and upper deck—and put a door in the side.

" 'Look! I am going to cover the earth with a flood and destroy every living being—everything in which there is the breath of life. All will die. But I promise to keep you safe in the ship, with your wife and your sons and their wives. Bring a pair of every animal—a male and a female—into the boat with you, to keep them alive through the flood. Bring in a pair of each kind of bird and animal and reptile. Store away in the boat all the food that they and you will need.' And Noah did everything as God commanded him.

"Finally the day came when the Lord said to Noah, 'Go into the boat with all your family, for among all the people of the earth, I consider you alone to be righteous. Bring in the animals, too—a pair of each, except those kinds I have chosen for eating and for sacrifice; take seven pairs of each of them, and seven pairs of every kind of bird. Thus there will be every kind of life reproducing again after the flood has ended. One week from today I will begin forty days and nights of rain; and all the animals and birds and reptiles I have made will die.'

"So Noah did everything the Lord commanded him. He was 600 years old when the flood came. He boarded the boat with his wife and sons and their wives, to escape the flood. With him were all the various kinds of animals—those for eating and sacrifice, and those that were not, and the birds and reptiles. They came into the boat in pairs, male and female, just as God commanded Noah.

"One week later, when Noah was 600 years, two months, and seventeen days old, the rain came down in mighty torrents from the sky, and the subterranean waters burst forth upon the earth for forty days and nights. But Noah had gone into the boat that very day with his wife and his sons, Shem, Ham, and Japheth, and their wives. With them in the boat were pairs of every kind of animal—domestic and wild—and reptiles and birds of every sort. Two by two they came, male and female, just as God had commanded. Then the Lord God closed the door and shut them in.

"For forty days the roaring floods prevailed, covering the ground and lifting the boat high above the earth. As the water rose higher and higher above the ground, the boat floated safely upon it; until finally the water covered all the high mountains under the whole heaven, standing twenty-two feet and more above the highest peaks. And all living things upon the earth perished—birds, domestic and wild animals, and reptiles and all mankind—everything that breathed and lived upon dry land. All existence on the earth was blotted out—man and animals alike, and reptiles and birds. God destroyed them all, leaving only Noah alive, and those with him in the boat. And the water covered the earth 150 days.

"God didn't forget about Noah and all the animals in the boat: He sent a wind to blow across the waters, and the floods began to disappear, for the subterranean water sources ceased their gushing, and the torrential rains subsided. So the flood gradually receded until, 150 days after it began, the boat came to rest upon the mountains of Ararat. Three months later, as the waters continued to go down, other mountain peaks appeared.

"After another forty days, Noah opened a porthole and released a raven that flew back and forth until the earth was dry. Meanwhile he sent out a dove to see if it could find dry ground, but the dove found no place to light, and returned to Noah, for the water was still too high. So Noah held out his hand and drew the dove back into the boat.

"Seven days later Noah released the dove again, and this time, towards evening, the bird returned to him with an olive leaf in her beak. So Noah knew that the water was almost gone.

A week later he released the dove again, and this time she didn't come back.

"Twenty-nine days after that, Noah opened the door to look, and the water was gone. Eight more weeks went by. Then at last the earth was dry. Then God told Noah, 'You may all go out. Release all the animals, birds, and reptiles, so that they will breed abundantly and reproduce in great numbers.' So the boat was soon empty. Noah, his wife, and his sons and their wives all disembarked, along with all the animals, reptiles, and birds—all left the ark in pairs and groups.

"Then Noah built an altar and sacrificed on it some of the animals and birds God had designated for that purpose. And Jehovah was pleased with the sacrifice and said to himself, 'I will never do it again—I will never again curse the earth, destroying all living things, even though man's bent is always toward evil from his earliest youth, and even though he does such wicked things. As long as the earth remains, there will be springtime and harvest, cold and heat, winter and summer, day and night.' "

Thus ends the Flood account as recorded in the book of Genesis.

It is probable that all the traditions of the great Flood in existence today reflect the same basic worldwide catastrophe relayed initially by members of Noah's family. The famed Gilgamesh Epic is one of these. It is the Flood tradition as told by Gilgamesh, the legendary giant of the Babylonians. It seems unlikely that Noah would be the sole survivor to tell the story of his family's survival.

The modern story of the discovery of the ancient epic had its beginning in the 1850's when a team of British archaeologists unearthed the clay-tablet library of King Ashurbanipal in Nineveh above the banks of the river Tigris. Not until years later, however, shortly before the turn of the century, was the value of the cuneiform tablets revealed. Written in ancient Akkadian, they related the story of the legendary Babylonian hero, Gilgamesh. Through further study it was shown that his epic really was not a unique item, "but that it belonged to the rich heritage of all the great nations of the ancient East. Hittites and Egyptians translated it into their own tongues, and cuneiform tablets discovered by the Nile still show clearly the marks in red ink opposite those parts which Egyptian scribes found difficult to translate.

"At last a little clay fragment gave the clue to the origin of the Epic of Gilgamesh. The world owes its original composition to the Sumerians, the people whose capital stood on the site of Ur."[4]

The clue to what might be contained in the more than 20,000 clay tablets uncovered in Ashurbanipal's palace presented itself when the British orientalist George Smith began the task of sorting and deciphering the first batch of tablets. Appointed to the painstaking job of copying the various inscriptions, he gradually obtained a thorough working knowledge of the cuneiform script. "While engaged at this task, he accidentally came across a small fragment of a tablet on which he read these words, 'The mountain of Nisir stopped the ship. . . . I sent forth a dove and it left. The dove went and turned, and a resting place it did not find, and it returned.'

"Smith perceived at once that these lines resembled an incident in the account of the Flood of Noah as recorded in Genesis, and he began an untiring search for the missing fragments. His labors were rewarded beyond expectation. He found not only many fragments of this account of the Flood but parts of two other copies."[5]

Now, nearly a century later, foremost Semitic scholars generally agree that the date of the composition of the Gilgamesh Epic must have been approximately 2,000 years B.C., several centuries before Moses penned his account in Genesis.

The actual Deluge section of the Epic is preceded by the account of a man called Gilgamesh, who, in order to ensure his immortality, decided to embark on a long and perilous journey to find his ancestor Utnapishtim, whom he had been told possessed the secrets of immortal life granted to him as a special favor by the gods.

"Please tell me the Secret of Life," Gilgamesh pleaded after finally locating him. Utnapishtim, moved with compassion, related to him the story of the Flood. Recalling that he once lived in Shuruppak as a worshipper of the true god Ea, he revealed to Gilgamesh that at one time in history the gods had decided to destroy mankind by a great waterflood and that he had been warned by Ea to prepare for this great destruction.

In free translation, the story reads as follows:

Gilgamesh said to Utnapishtim the Distant,

"Looking at you, Utnapishtim, I find that you are really not different at all. In fact, you're very much like I am. I had you pictured quite differently; someone specially made for doing battle, but you are like me. You too lie on your side and your back.

"Tell me, how did you really manage to land among the company of the gods and receive everlasting life?"

"Gilgamesh, I will tell you a secret," Utnapishtim answered. "It is a secret of the gods—listen.

"You know the city of Shuruppak? You know it is located on the banks of the river Euphrates. Well, that city was already old and the gods lived there among the people when a great god decided to have a flood.

"Anu was there, and Enlil, the war-counselor, and Ninurta, their representative and Ennugi, their vizier. Even Ninigiku was there.

"And he said,

" 'Reed hut, and walls, listen and consider! You man of Shuruppak, you son of Ubara-Tutu!

" 'Tear down your house and build a ship. Leave all your possessions behind and save your life. Leave your goods behind.

You are in danger. You've got to go into a ship with representatives of all of the living creatures.

" 'But first, you'll have to build the ship, and I want you to do it according to these specifications:

" 'The length of the ship shall be equal to its width!'

"I understood him perfectly and said to Ea, the god,

" 'Surely, Lord. I will do what you have told me to do. I will honor your command, but what am I going to tell the people in the city and the elders?'

"Ea opened his mouth and answered,

" 'This is what you will tell them. Just say that I have found out that they hate me and that they no longer want me to live with them. Just tell them that you don't want to live with them either because of that and that you will go down to the apsu and live with god.

" 'Tell them that I will bring a flood of water down upon them!'

"Soon thereafter I began to build the ship. Help came from everywhere. Children brought pitch, while the grown-ups brought other materials. Five days after Ea spoke to me, I laid the keel. I made the floor space one iku in size and the walls of the ship one hundred twenty cubits long. I designed it and divided the ship into six decks, giving it a total of seven stories.

"Then I looked at the ground plan and divided it into nine sections, after which I drove water stoppers into the holes. Next I gathered punting poles and stored up a supply of food. But that wasn't all: To make it waterproof, I poured six shar of pitch into the furnace and three shar of asphalt and three shar of oil. Besides this, it took a shar of oil to saturate the water stoppers and two shar of oil for the boatman.

"It took much to feed the laborers. I slaughtered cows and sheep day after day, and they drank so much oil and wine that it seemed as if it were water.

"But on New Year's day, the ship was finished and it caused

a great celebration. I washed my hands; the job of building the ship had been a hard one.

"Hurriedly I gathered all my silver and gold and stashed it on the ship, and after I had put all my relatives aboard, I took representatives of all living creatures in the field into the ship and also took the craftsman.

"Shamash had given me a definite time.

"And in the evening, the sender of the storm started the rains to start. I looked at it and became frightened. I walked into the ship and shut and door behind me, and told Pazur-Amurri, the navigator, to take good care of the ship.

"Early the next morning, the first shimmer of the day was obscured by an ominous black thundercloud, and while the gods Shullat and Hanish announced the tragedy to come, Irragal's force pulled out our mast, and Ninurta's anger breached the dikes. The flashing light of Anunnaki illuminated the thundering skies while the raging of Adad could be heard all over the heavens.

"Then—darkness. All light disappeared; the land shook and broke like a pot. A whole day long the tempest raged. Like a battle it covered the people, and no one could see his neighbor. Not even heaven could recognize the people. So awesome was the spectacle that even the gods became frightened and terror stricken. In confusion they fled and ascended to the heaven of Anu and there cowered like dogs. . . .

"Ishtar, the lovely voiced lady of the gods lamented like a woman in labor.

" 'The things of old have turned to clay,' she cried in anguish, 'because I advocated bad things in the presence of the gods. It is my fault that this is happening. How could I do such a thing. My people are being destroyed, and like the spawn of the fish they now float on the waves.'

"And the Anunnaki-gods cried with her. They sat down and let their heads hang low, and they cried and cried. . . .

"And for six days and six nights the winds continued, and the rains kept coming down, and the flood that resulted covered the land, but on the seventh day of the terrible storm, the flood which had covered everything like a devouring army, grew quiet, and the storm stopped and the flood waters became quiet.

"I looked at the sea and everything was still . . . and all the people had become dust.

"I went to the roof and opened a porthole and the sunlight touched my face and I bowed my head and sat down and cried —and the tears ran down my face.

"I looked at the horizon trying to find the end of the ocean, but it was not until 48 hours later that I saw the first sign of land. It was Mount Nisir, and when we reached it, it held us fast. It did not let us go again.

"Six long days the mountain held on to us and on the seventh day I decided to let a dove go, but soon she returned to me, for she had not been able to find a resting place.

"Next I sent out a swallow, but she too came back, for she too could not find a resting place.

"And then I sent the raven, and when she saw that the waters were going down she flew around for a while, cawed and took off. After that I let all the birds go and offered a sacrifice.

"I took refreshments to the peak of the mountain in seven kettles, and used sweet cane, cedar, and myrtle for firewood, and when the gods smelled that they gathered like flies over the sacrifice.

"Then the great goddess arrived and lifted up the great jewels which Anu had made for her and proclaimed,

" 'Listen, you gods who are assembled here, as surely as I shall not forget the jewels around my neck, so surely I will remember these days and will never forget them. Come and accept the sacrifice—all of you except Enlil, for he caused this deluge without any consideration, and caused my people to be destroyed.'

"Enlil was angry when he arrived and screamed,

" 'Has anyone escaped the flood? No one was supposed to live through it!'

"Ninurta looked at him and said to Enlil,

" 'How could you expect to do a thing like this without the approval of Ea? Only he understands these things!'

"Then Ea said,

" 'Oh, Enlil, how could you do a thing like this? Sure, the sinner is guilty, but you cannot be too severe. Instead of a deluge, why didn't you send a lion to punish them? Or a wolf instead of the flood? In fact, why didn't you send a lion and have him punish humanity? Or why not a famine?'

"And Ea turned and took me by the hand and went with me into the ship. And with my wife kneeling down at my side, he touched our foreheads and blessed us and said,

" 'Up to this moment, Utnapishtim, you have been a mere mortal, but from now on both you and your wife will be like gods among us. From now on you will live in the far distance at the mouth of the rivers. There, Utnapishtim, you shall dwell.'

"And so I joined the gods, and they made me live among them at the mouth of the rivers."

A fable? A mere myth? The ancient scribes who faithfully copied the words of this narrative surely did not feel that way, even though the Babylonians, Assyrians, Hittites, and Egyptians who translated all or part into their own words never had actual proof that they were dealing with a realistic historical event. Reading this account, however, leaves one with the impression that this could be the story of a man describing his own experiences, his own heartbreak. Could someone who had not been a part of this calamitous destruction have described the awesome scenes with such pathos and feeling?

Utnapishtim might have been the Biblical Noah.

It is not difficult to imagine that the discovery of the epic caused much skepticism, but also tremendous concern among historians and theologians. Critics soon embarked on feverish attempts to prove that the Biblical account was based on ideas borrowed from this Babylonian myth. It must be admitted that there are striking similarities between the two traditions. These general areas of agreement cannot be ignored.

Frederick A. Filby writes in *The Flood Reconsidered,* "The story of the Flood seems to have been so well known that it became one of the popular 'books' in the ancient cuneiform libraries, and fragments of a number of slightly different texts are known. One broken fragment from Sumeria speaks of the Flood sweeping over the land and 'tossing the huge boat about.' It tells how 'Ziusudra the king, the Preserver of the seed of mankind . . . opened a window of the huge boat.' Several similar fragments were referred to by Prof. Kramer and in two of these we are told that the Flood 'wiped out everything.'

"A small fragment discovered at Nippur and undoubtedly of very early date speaks of a flood 'sweeping away all mankind at once and of someone building a 'great ship . . . with a strong roof' in which vessel 'beasts of the field, the birds of heaven and the family' were saved."[6]

After careful comparison of the two major accounts—the Bible story and the Gilgamesh Epic—Merril F. Unger points out that

(a) Both accounts state that the Deluge was divinely planned.

(b) Both accounts agree that the impending catastrophe was divinely revealed to the hero of the Deluge.

(c) Both connect the Deluge with the defection of the human race.

(d) Both tell of the deliverance of the hero and his family.

(e) Both assert that the hero of the Deluge was divinely instructed to build a huge boat to preserve life.

(f) Both indicate the physical causes of the Flood.

(g) Both specify the duration of the Flood, although differing in the elapsed time.

(h) Both name the landing place of the boat.

(i) Both tell of the sending forth of birds at certain intervals to ascertain the decrease of waters.

(j) Both describe acts of worship by the hero after his deliverance.

(k) Both allude to the bestowment of special blessings upon the hero after the disaster.[7]

In his book *The Flood,* Alfred Rehwinkel writes: "According to both accounts, the Flood is brought on because the earth was full of violence. In both cases dimensions of the ship are given, though differing in details. In both cases representatives of all animals are taken into the ark. In the Babylonian account the Flood lasts seven days. In the Bible narrative the embarkation takes seven days. In both cases a raven and a dove are sent forth from the ark. The Babylonian accounts add a swallow. . . . The rainbow of Genesis is represented by the great jewels of Ishtar. In both there is a covenant guaranteeing that no world Flood is ever to come upon the earth again to destroy it."[8]

Alexander Heidel, on the other hand, has carefully analyzed a number of important *differences* between the two stories and has concluded that even though there are definite areas of agreement, these areas seem to be caused by the two accounts having been based on the same *event,* not the same *account.*[9]

There are also other Deluge traditions equally as significant as the Gilgamesh Epic, and they, too, point toward a common *event,* not necessarily the same traditional account. Berosus, a contemporary of Alexander the Great and Babylonian high priest of the temple Bel-Murduk writes in *The Chaldean History:*

"In this year, the God Bel revealed to Xisuthrus in a dream that in the fifteenth year and the month of Daesius there would be a great storm of rain, and man would be destroyed by the flood of waters. He made him bury all written records, medieval, and modern, in Sippara, the City of the Sun, and build a ship and embark in it with his kindred and nearest friends. He was also to take food and drink into the ship, and carry into it all creatures, winged and four-footed.

"Xisuthrus did as he was bidden and built a boat fifteen stadia long and two stadia in breadth, and placed in it his wife and child, his relatives and friends. Then the inundation came. When the rain ceased, Xisuthrus sent out some birds, but they returned to the ship, as they could find nothing to eat and no place to rest. After a few days he sent out other birds. They also returned, but with mud on their feet. When Xisuthrus sent yet others, and they never returned, Xisuthrus knew that the earth had appeared. He took out a part of the roof of his boat and perceived that it had settled down on a mountain. Then he went out with his wife and daughter and the architect of the boat. He worshipped the earth, and built an altar and offered sacrifice to the gods, and then disappeared, together with those whom he had brought out of the boat. When his companions whom he had left in the boat had gone out and were in search of Xisuthrus, his voice called to them out of the air, saying that the gods had carried him away in reward for his piety; that he with his daughter and the architect were dwelling among the gods. But the others were to return from Armenia where they were, to Babylon, and, in obedience to the command of the gods, dig up the books buried at Sippara and give them to mankind. They obeyed these instructions. They sacrificed to the gods and returned by land to Babylon. They dug up the sacred books, erected many cities and returned to Babylon."

Berosus added to the story: "There are, they say, remains of the ship in Armenia on the mountains of the Cordyaeans, where local people take pieces of asphalt from the object and use these for amulets against danger and catastrophies."[10]

In two more Assyro-Babylonian accounts, the Epic of Sesit and the Epic of Atrahasis, most of the elements already known from the Gilgamesh Epic are used, and they agree in general with the major line of the story. The more traditional classical historians also have mentioned the existence of Noah's ark.

Flavius Josephus, the Jewish historian of the early years of our Christian era, indicated that in his time, too, there were rumors that the remains of the ark could still be seen.

In his *Antiquities of the Jews,* he wrote:

"Then the Ark landed on a mountaintop in Armenia." "The Armenians call that spot the landingplace, for it was there that the ark came safe to land, and they show the relics of it even today.

"This flood and the ark are mentioned by all who have written histories of the barbarians," he continues, "and among these is Berosus the Chaldean who in his description of the events of the flood writes somewhere as follows: 'It is said, moreover, that portions of the vessel still survive in Armenia on the mountain of the Cordyaeans, and that persons carry off pieces of the bitumen which they use as talismans.'

"These matters are also mentioned by Hyronimus the Egyptian," Josephus goes on, "the author of 'Ancient History of Phoenicia,' by Mnaseas and many others. Nicolaus of Damascus in his ninety-sixth book relates the story as follows: 'There is above the country of Minnaeus in Armenia a great mountain called Baris on which, as the story goes, many refugees found safety at the time of the flood and one man transported upon an ark, grounded upon the summit and relics of the timber were for a long time preserved. This might well be the same man about whom Moses the lawgiver of the Jews spoke.' "

At the end of the chapter where Josephus describes the Deluge he added a short note:

"Now I have for witness to what I have said all those that have written antiquities, both among the Greeks and the barbarians. For even Manetho, who wrote the Egyptian History, and Berosus who collected the Chaldean Monuments, and Mochus and Hestiaeus, and besides these Hieronymus the Egyptian, and those who composed the Phoenician History agree to what I say. Hesiod also, and Hecataeus, and Hellanicus, and Aculsilaus; and besides these Ephorus and Nicolaus relate that the ancients lived a thousand years."[11]

Flavius Josephus is not the only Christian era historian who has written about the ark. Six other historians beginning with St. Theophilus of Antioch in A.D. 120 follow the same, by now, traditional line. St. Theophilus writes essentially a similar account as Josephus; but Ephiphanus, Bishop of Salamis (A.D. 380) states insistently that the wood of Noah's ark is still being shown in the land of the Kurds (Armenia). These and other historical accounts must have been taken literally by Emperor Heraclius (A.D. 600), for in *History of the Saracenes,* Hussein El Macin of Bagdad states that the emperor *visited* the remains of the ark after he had destroyed the Persians in the city of Thenia, located near the foot of Mount Ararat.

Slightly more than 600 years after the emperor's visit the Armenian historian and world traveler Haithon writes that in the snow of Mount Ararat one can see a black spot which is Noah's ark, *which he himself saw in 1254.*

Even the renowned explorer Marco Polo (A.D. 1234-1324) writes in his *Travels:*

"And you should know that in this land of Armenia, the ark of Noah still rests on top of a certain great mountain where the snow stays so long that no one can climb it. The snow never melts—it gets thicker with each snowfall."

The collection of ancient Mideast reports dealing with the presence of the ark on the top of Mount Ararat is impressive, yet the historians who reported on it were all *from* the Mesopotamia and Palestine areas. The major accounts were written by men who spent their lives in the cradle of civilization; historians who grew up with not only historical accounts of the tragedy but with its folklore as well.

This, of course, has given rise to the idea that the Flood as described in the Bible and other sources might merely have been a local occurrence, large enough, however, to create the impression in primitive minds that it had indeed covered the entire globe. This is a vital issue; for if the Flood described in the Bible had been only an event of local importance, then Noah might have built his ship too small or too flimsy to withstand the elements of the ages. If, on the other hand, it had been constructed to resist the effects of an unlimited deluge, then the odds in favor of finding its remnants would be far greater. Also, if the flood had merely been a local one, then the traditions relating the events of the limited catastrophe would more likely be confined to the geographical area of the Middle East, inasmuch as it would have been of interest and importance only to those tribes and nations living in the general vicinity of the destructive flood.

There is no possible way for a universal flood to have occurred without leaving traces in the annals of human memory the world over, for not only must traditions and history reflect this tragedy, but the earth itself must reflect a visible impression of it. The world could hardly have experienced a devastation of such magnitude without bearing the scars.

REFERENCES

1. Genesis 7:11-24, Smith and Goodspeed.
2. *Gilgamesh Epic,* (lines 128-137) free translation.
3. Genesis 8:4, Smith and Goodspeed.
4. Werner Keller, *The Bible as History,* page 34.
5. Alfred M. Rehwinkel, *The Flood,* page 154.
6. Frederick A. Filby, *The Flood Reconsidered,* pages 41, 42.
7. Merril F. Unger, *Archaeology and the Old Testament,* third ed., pages 55-65.
8. Rehwinkel, *op. cit.,* p. 162.
9. *The Gilgamesh Epic and Old Testament Parallel,* second ed., pages 224-258.
10. Cory, *Old Fragments,* page 26; see also *Chronographia,* George Syncellus, pages 29, 30.
11. Flavius Josephus, *Antiquities of the Jews.*

CHAPTER 2

With a broad smile and a warm handshake, Dr. Smith welcomed me into his home in Greensboro, North Carolina, one balmy autumn evening in 1949, roughly ten years before our final sad farewell in his sickroom. For months now he and I on different continents had been engaged in some basic ark research. Now that he had invited me over to "come and share" the results of our months of work, I gladly accepted.

Digging into the past of ancient tribes and nations, *not* with a piercing spade but via myths and legends, is one of the most fascinating aspects of archaeology. Probing into mankind's silent memory, scouting for the almost forgotten legends and traditions that tend to substantiate and verify the Bible story of the Flood is even more of a challenge. Sharing our experiences and information gleaned from the great libraries of the United States and Europe, as well as insights gained from the study of Semitic languages, it had to be profitable for both of us.

A diligent researcher, Aaron Smith never doubted the outcome of our combined effort, especially since it dealt with trying to uncover material that would vindicate the Biblical ark story.

Seated in his cozily furnished living room in front of a crackling fire, he pointed to a neatly stacked pile of papers on the end table, an arm's length from his chair.

"That's where it all is, Rene," he said, smiling with an inner warmth that betrayed his deep satisfaction. "I've come across nearly eighty legends and traditions, *all* of which deal with a flood. Even though every one of them stands out because of specific differences, they all share the same basic story—that of a catastrophe which destroyed all of mankind except just a few who escaped. This one, however, varies slightly," and slowly he extracted a yellowed folder from an attaché case leaning against his chair.

"Several documents belonging to some of this country's leading secret religious organizations make mention of a tradition that sheds a new light on our search," he said. "They claim they have documentary evidence that the body of Adam was embalmed and handed down from father to son, and that it was finally delivered by Lamech into the hands of Noah. Furthermore they assert that Noah took the body of Adam with him into the ark and that he prayed daily to God in the presence of Adam's body."

Opening the file, he handed me a number of handwritten pages.

"These are copied passages from the so-called 'Forgotten Books of Eden,'" he explained. "Even though this material is not supported by reliable historians, it does shed an interesting light on what might have taken place in those early years."

I opened the folder and read:

"Therefore, O my sons, set your hearts on your own selves, and keep the commandment of God which is with you. And when you go from this holy mountain into a strange land which ye know not, take with you the body of our father Adam, and with it these three precious gifts and offerings, namely the gold, the incense, and the myrrh; and let them be in the place where the body of our father Adam shall lie.

"And unto him of you who shall be left, O my sons, shall the Word of God come, and when he goes out of this land he shall take with him the body of our father Adam, and shall lay it in the middle of the earth, the place in which salvation shall be wrought.

"Then Noah said unto him, 'Who is he of us that shall be left?' And Jared answered, 'Thou art he that shall be left. And thou shalt take the body of our father Adam from the cave, and place it with thee in the ark when the flood comes. And thy son Shem, who shall come out of thy loins, he it is who shall lay the body of our father Adam in the middle of the earth, in the place whence salvation shall come.'

"Then Jared turned to his son, Enoch, and said unto him, 'Thou, my son, abide in this cave, and minister diligently before the body of our father Adam all the days of thy life; and feed thy people in righteousness and innocence.' "[1]

Quietly Aaron Smith waited until I had digested the information. Then he looked at me.

"This surely makes the search for the ark even more fascinating, doesn't it?" he asked. "While we have no evidence whatsoever that this tradition is backed by facts—and the Bible doesn't mention it—it nevertheless adds a new element of suspense to the search."

Putting the folder aside, he reached for the stack of research material; then, adding my files to his, we commenced to work, comparing and evaluating the traditions and myths that traced the flood story to many distant lands.

It is a little-known fact that over the years approximately 80,000 books[2] pertaining to the Deluge have been written in seventy-six different languages—and these are only the ones that can be traced through the card indexes of the great libraries of the world. Many more have no doubt been started, edited, and written but never catalogued. Most of these are concerned with the archaeological and geological aspects and not with the legends and folklore underlying the basic history of the ancient civilizations. Yet these tales are of the utmost importance, as their very existence among widely separated tribes is what generally might be expected if the Flood was indeed a universal one.

Famed German researcher, Dr. Johannes Riem, stated in the introduction to his book, *Die Sintflut in Sage und Wissenshaft,* a major work on flood legends:

"Among all traditions there is none so general, so widespread on earth, and so apt to show what may develop from the same material according to the varying spiritual character of a people as the flood tradition. Lengthy and thorough discussions with Dr. Kunike have convinced me of the evident correctness of his position that the fact of the Deluge is granted because at the basis of all myths, particularly nature myths, there is a real fact, but during a subsequent period the material was given its present mythical character and form."[3]

Other well-known scholars support Dr. Riem's point of view. The Scottish geologist of the last century, Hugh Miller, after having carefully examined the original of the world's most important traditions, concluded,

"There is, however, *one special tradition* which seems to be more deeply impressed and more widely spread than any of the others. The destruction of *well-nigh the whole human race,* in an early age of the world's history, *by a great deluge,* appears to have so impressed the minds of the few survivors, and seems to have been handed down to their children, in consequence, with *such terror-struck impressiveness* that their remote descendants of the present day have not even yet forgotten it. It appears in almost every mythology, and lives in the most distant countries, and among the most barbarous tribes. It was the laudable ambition of Humboldt, first entertained at a very early period of life, to penetrate into distant regions, unknown to the natives of Europe at that time, that he might acquaint himself in fields of research altogether fresh and new, with men and with nature in their most primitive conditions. In carrying out his design, he journeyed far into the woody wilderness that surrounds the Orinoco and found himself among tribes of wild Indians whose very names were unknown to the civilized world. And yet *among even these forgotten races* of the human family he found the tradition of the deluge *still fresh and distinct;* not confined to a single tribe, but general among the scattered nations of that great region, and intertwined with curious additions, suggestive of the inventions of classic mythology of the Old World."[4] (Italics supplied.)

In his book Dr. Riem furnished us with a world map indicating the various spots on the globe where he discovered deluge traditions. Interestingly enough, most of the traditions he located were found in Asia and on the North American continent; however, Australia and Europe, together with Africa and the South Sea Islands, were also found to have their own individual traditions.

It is obviously impossible to list even briefly all the pertinent legends and traditions; yet in order to show the similarity in their general character, the highlights of the accumulated flood mythology as discovered in different parts of the world should be aired.

Some of the most striking deluge traditions are found in Asia and in China in particular, where it is told that a tremendous flood of devastating force occurred around 2300 B.C. According to this story, the flood, caused by an overflow of the great rivers, was stopped by the swelling of the sea. Fah-he, the Chinese hero, escaped the destruction along with his wife, his three sons, and three daughters.

Additional legends found on the mainland of China maintain that all Chinese are direct descendants of an ancient ancestor of the Chinese people called "Nu-wah," who distinguished himself for overcoming a great flood. If this is true, then one would expect records and venerated traditions in China to show some connection with thoughts, religions, and experiences prevailing in the time of Noah.

Dr. E. W. Thwing, a researcher who spent many years in

China, uncovered just that. He stated to Dr. Aaron J. Smith that the most ancient of the Chinese records did indeed give a clear idea of one God, and that idolatry was a relatively rare concept which may have derived from some primitive revelation.

Another revealing point in connection with the Chinese story is that ancient Chinese writing has many words that can *only* be traced to "Nu-wah" and the Flood. The Chinese word for "righteousness," for example, is a combination of the pictorial symbols for "lamb" placed over a picture of "myself." This is very possibly related with Noah's desire to justify himself in the eyes of God as manifested in the burnt offering he made after departing from the ark.

Continuing his search into a probable connection between China and Noah, Dr. Thwing stated that "the Chinese have records and traditions of a great flood. And it is a curious fact that the word used for 'ship' as printed in Chinese books and papers today, is the very ancient character, made up of the picture of 'boat' and 'eight mouths,' showing that the first ship was a boat carrying eight persons.

"In looking over some old books of ancient stories and traditions, I found a story about the ancestor 'Nu-wah,' " he went on. "Interestingly enough, 'Nu' means 'woman' and 'wah' is 'flowery.' "[5] Thus this ancient one has been considered a *female ancestor*. However, in the old book it was noted that two small "mouth" characters were placed beside the name "Nu-wah," *indicating that the Chinese characters were not used for their meaning, but for their sound.* And so it was not a female ancestor, but an ancient man, famous in a flood, the sound of whose name was preserved as "Nu-wah."

This is further supported by indications found in the earliest part of Chinese history. There we notice many different accounts of the creation of the universe usually attributed to P'an-ku. Its catastrophic destruction and accompanying deluge is considered to be the deed of Jung-ku, but its reconstruction is credited to

Nu-wah. Later in the sequence came legendary monarchs and cultural heroes, sometimes mentioned as the Three Sovereigns (three sons of Noah?). These in turn were succeeded by the Three Dynasties, Hsia, Shang, and Chou, considered by scholars to initiate the historical period.

Can the Chinese Nu-wah and the Biblical Noah be synonymous?

The name Noah seems to have survived in many a tale. Depending on the pronunciation and the letter symbols used, each story utilizing that name may have a different spelling. Yet when pronounced, they have basically the same sound. Such is the case with the Hawaiian legend of Nu-u, the one righteous man. Long after the creation of Kumuhonua, the first man, the earth had become degenerate and wicked and had ceased to worship the true god. Cane, the great god, was highly displeased with the growing infidelity, and in utter disgust decided to destroy the world. Not wanting to begin his creation all over again, he decided to allow Nu-u, the only righteous man, and his family to escape the consequences of his wrath by making him build a great canoe called "Waa-halau" with a house on it. He told him to stock it with supplies for himself, his wife Lili-Noe, their children, and the animals he wanted him to take.

When the rains came and the waters rose and the oceans merged, the Waa-Halau drifted around for days on end, and while it drifted all mankind was destroyed.

When the torrential weather finally subsided and the waters receded, Nu-u looked around and noticed dry land and the moon shining about it in all its splendor. Mistaking it for the face of Cane, the great god, he fell down and worshiped it.

Watching Nu-u from on high, Cane became greatly displeased at this new sign of ungodliness and cast down a rainbow and rode down on it to reprimand Nu-u.

"Oh, great god," a terrified Nu-u explained, "I made a mistake —I beg forgiveness." Cane smiled and returned to heaven the same way he came, *but left the rainbow as token of his eternal forgiveness.* Together with his three sons Nu-u repopulated the earth.

Among the more than thirty flood legends found in the Orient, the Indonesians can lay claim to some of the most descriptive ones.

"The Battaks of Sumatra say that when the earth grew old and dirty, the Creator—whom they call Debata—sent a flood to destroy every living thing. Debata was angry. The last human pair had taken refuge, not in an ark, but on the top of the highest mountain, and the waters of the deluge had already reached their knees when Debata, the Lord of all, repented of his resolution to make an end of all mankind.

"Magnificently picturesque legends have grown up among the natives of Engano, an island to the west of Sumatra, and among the Sea Dyaks of Sarawak in Borneo. The Bugi-speaking Toradjas of the Central Celebes tell of a flood which covered the highest mountain, leaving bare only the tip of Mount Wawom Pebato. This time no lucky pair escaped. Instead, the only living creatures to survive the flood were a pregnant woman and a pregnant mouse."[6]

In many countries the flood traditions have been interwoven with nature myths, and animals have taken the place of the former human heroes, giving the historical tale an aura of child-like fantasy. The majority of flood stories told in Latin America seem to fall into this classification.

Once long ago in gray history, it is told around Peruvian camp-fires, an Indian took his llama to a rich green pasture. But despite his desperate attempts, he did not succeed in forcing the llama to stay. Great sorrow and anguish showed in the animal's eyes, and he even refused to eat.

"Eat, llama," his master commanded him. "I am giving you the best pasture in the land and yet you refuse to eat. What's wrong?"

"You're a fool," the llama replied to the surprised Indian. "You know there must be a powerful reason to keep me from eating. The gods have revealed to me that within five days the sea will rise up and cover all the land, except the highest mountaintop. I am sad because all humanity will die."

"Is there no way to escape?" the Indian cried.

"Yes, follow me with supplies for at least five days, and we will go to the highest mountaintop."

After hours of climbing, the llama and the Indian reached the top of Villca Coto where they joined the host of birds and animals that had preceded them in seeking refuge. Scarcely had they reached the summit when the rains came down and the sea began to rise. With relentless fury the sea's angry waves covered the villages and hillsides and gnawed at everything within reach. Then it began to cover Villca Coto! For a few hours it seemed as though it would cover the very top, as it had already reached the fox's tail. But just then the five-day period ended, and the waters had to recede. On the sixth day the waters had already diminished so far that the llama and the Indian were able to recognize some landmarks. But in between them everything was dead. All men lay dead, their bodies floating on the receding waves.

Then the llama said mournfully, "You have witnessed the end of your world, Indian. Now you have to repopulate the earth." Sadly the Indian left Villca Coto.

Another South American tribe, the Carayas Indians of the wild Amazon region of Brazil, tell their flood story known as "the tale of the calabash."

One day, the story goes, the Indians decided to hunt the animals of the forest. After having killed many wild pigs, they dug into the ground and found a deer, a tapir, then a white deer, and finally they discovered a man's foot.

Frightened, they called upon their wizard Anatina who unearthed the entire man by simply singing, "I am Anatina, and

I want you to bring me some tobacco." Having never seen a man smoking, the Carayas did not understand what he was doing and offered him fruit, flowers, nuts, and grains of the fields. Only when he showed them the man smoking did they understand him and proceeded to bring him tobacco. Hour after hour he smoked until he lost consciousness. In triumph the Carayas dragged him to their village where he woke up, singing.

Wild-eyed, he began stalking the Carayas until they all ran away terrified. Racing after them, he managed to grab several calabashes filled with water. When they refused to stop, he broke one, then another one, and still another. Every time a calabash broke, the water leaked out and made the rivers rise higher and higher until the whole country was flooded except for the mountain Tapirapis where all the Carayas had taken refuge.

"Fish of the waters, help me," Anatina pleaded. "Drag the Carayas into the water." But it was to no avail. Nothing could pull the frightened Carayas off the mountain; that is, not until the call of Anatina was heard by the bicudo fish. Without alerting the Carayas, he climbed the backside of the mountain, and with his long beak pulled the Indians off and threw them into the rushing waters.

Only two Indians survived by holding fast to the high peak of the mountain. There they remained until the waters receded; then they repopulated the region.

North America, with its many Indian tribes, also has its share of flood legends, *forty-six of which deal with a universal flood story*. Sherman Coolidge, a member of the Arapaho tribe, tells the following tale, highly revered by the tribe:

"Long ago before there was any animal life on earth," he says, "the entire surface of the planet was covered with water, except the top of one high mountain. Upon this mountain sat a lone Arapaho, poor, weeping, and in great distress. The Great Spirit saw him and felt sorry for him, and in his pity sent three ducks down to the poor Indian. The Arapaho ordered the ducks to dive down into the waters and bring up some dirt. The first and second tried, but after remaining under water for a long time, each returned without any dirt. Then the third went down and was gone so long that the surface of the water where he disappeared had become still and quiet. The Arapaho believed his duck to be dead when suddenly she returned to the surface with some dirt in her bill. As soon as the Arapaho received this bit of dirt, the waters began to subside.

"In a short time the waters had receded so far that they could not be seen from the top of the highest mountains, but this Arapaho, who was endowed with supernatural wisdom and power, knew that they surrounded the earth, even as they do to this day. The Arapaho, who had been saved by the ducks, then became the sole possessor of the land. He made the rivers and made the trees to grow and then the buffaloes, elks, deer, and other animals, all the birds of the air and the fishes in the water and all the trees and bushes and all other things that can be grown by planting seed in the ground."[7]

Being true nature people, the early inhabitants of America had a legend fitting every occasion, and the deluge-escape story was one that could not be suppressed.

The Athapascan Indians living in the western part of the United States have a tradition wherein the gods have taken upon themselves to repair the sky which threatens to fall. Having accomplished that, they caused an unending rain to fall upon the earth below.

"Every day it rained, every night it rained. All the people slept. The sky fell, the land was not. For a very great distance there was no land. The waters of the oceans came together. Animals of all kinds drowned. Where the waters went, there were no trees. There was no land. Water came, they say. The waters completely joined everywhere. Trees and grass were not. There were no fish or land animals or birds. Human beings and animals alike had been washed away. The wind did not blow through the portals of the world, nor was there snow, nor frost, nor rain. It did not thunder, nor did it lightnen. Since there were no trees to be struck, it did not thunder. There were neither clouds nor fog, nor was there sun. It was very dark. Then it was that this earth with its great, long horns got up and walked away down this way from the north. As it walked along through the deep places, the water rose to its shoulders. When it came up into shallower places, it looked up. There is a ridge in the north upon which the waves break. When it came to the middle of the world in the east under the rising of the sun, it looked up again. Then where it looked up will be a large land near to the coast. Far away to the south it continued, looking up. It walked under the ground. Having come from the north, it traveled far south and laid [sic] down. Nagaitsche, standing on earth's head, had been carried to the south. Where earth laid [sic] down, Nagaitsche placed its head as it should be and spread gray clay between its eyes on each horn. Upon the clay he placed a layer of reeds and then another layer of clay. In this he placed upright blue grass, brush, and trees. 'I have finished,' he said. 'Let there be mountain peaks here on its head. Let the waves of the sea break against them.' "[8]

And thus the earth was made new.

One of the most descriptive legends relating to the Flood story originates from the Transylvania region of Rumania where the Gypsies still tell with awe the age-old "tale of the fish."

According to their flood version, there was a time when man was happy, without a care in the world and assured of eternal life. Both animals and humans lived together in great harmony, and no evil deed was committed for fear of losing their happy home.

For thousands of years this continued, and sin never entered until that fateful day when a mysterious old man knocked at the door of an elderly couple's house and asked for a night's lodging.

Early the next morning, as the guest prepared to leave, he turned toward his host.

"Here's a vessel with a fish," he said. "I want to leave this with you. Whatever you do, don't eat it. Don't ever eat it! Just take care of it, and if you can do this for nine days, I will return and reward you greatly."

Having said that, he disappeared.

Realizing that *she* had not promised the stranger that she would honor his request, the woman tried to find ways to change her husband's mind about protecting the fish.

"I want it for supper," she said. "I didn't promise anything, so I can eat it."

The squabble that followed caused the first sin to enter this beautiful creation. Finally the woman vowed that she would not kill the little fish. "So help me God."

Feeling certain that the danger was past, the husband left the house. However, barely had he done so when the woman grabbed the fish out of the bowl and placed it on the hot coals. The effect was disastrous. Fierce shafts of lightning stabbed into the little house, and a roar of thunder enveloped her as she fell dead to the ground. Ominous black clouds covered the house, and the rainstorm that followed flooded the river until the water spilled onto the banks. And still it rained and rained.

On the ninth day, the strange old man returned and gently put his arm around his host.

"You did not kill the fish, my son," he said sadly. "It was your wife. Take another wife and put her and your family into a big boat in order to save yourself, for this rain will continue for a long, long time. Make room in the boat for animals and plants as well, for everything that is touched by the great flood will die. All creatures will die in the flood."

For a year the rains continued to drench the earth, and the only things that could be seen were the sky and the waters. Even the birds were gone; they had all perished in the rains.

It took a full year for the rains to stop and the waters to subside and for the man and his family to leave the boat. But now a different world was waiting for him. Gone was eternal life. Gone was the civilization that had existed before the flood. Labor and sorrow were now to be his steady companions, and sickness and death were to be his closest friends.

The Romans and the Greeks have still other flood legends, but they all point toward the same underlying cause.

As might be expected, "all these traditions have been modified through the ages," Alfred Rehwinkel comments in *The Flood*. "They have been influenced by the customs of various people and by the environment in which they are found and thus have taken on local color and sometimes extravagant and fantastic proportions, so that the kernel of truth in many cases is seriously obscured. And yet, when stripped of the accretions which have accumulated as they were handed down from father to son through the generations, the essential facts of the great catastrophe are easily discernible. There is almost complete agreement among them all on the three main features: 1. There is a universal destruction of the human race and all other living things by water. 2. An ark, or boat, is provided as the means of escape. 3. A seed of mankind is preserved to perpetuate the human race. To these might be added a fourth, which, though not occurring in all the traditions, occurs very frequently, namely that the wickedness of man is given as the cause of the Flood."[9]

One of the most perplexing problems in the entire search for ark evidence is the almost total absence of hard and tangible information concerning the ark within the confines of the Armenian community. This is rather strange, inasmuch as the Armenians have done considerable research into Biblical history, especially where it touched the physical land area covered by the Armenian nation.

Their interest dates back to A.D. 301, at which time Christianity received a tremendous push when it was officially proclaimed as the national religion of Armenia. In one move, King Tiridates of Armenia, together with the nobility of the country, were baptized by St. Gregory the Illuminator, thereby making Armenia the first Christian nation in the world. From that moment it was forced to fight for its new religion, but it survived.

Roughly one hundred years later, the invention of the Armenian alphabet enabled that country's scholars to record not only their history but existing Christian traditions as well. During those years the Bible and numerous works written by the early church fathers were meticulously translated into Armenian from Syrian and Greek. Comments the Armenian writer Assadour Antreassian, "It is for this reason that the fifth century is called the golden age of the Armenian nation."

The only plausible explanation for the near total absence of Ararat information and traditions is most likely due to the attempts to annihilate the Armenian nation, the first time occurring during the first world war when more than a million and a half Armenians were killed; and in 1920 when the results were equally as tragic. How severe these efforts were can be judged from the fact that simultaneously hundreds of churches, monasteries, convents, and libraries were burned to the ground. Hundreds of thousands of historical volumes were destroyed. That some records still survived seems a miracle in itself. The nonexistence of knowledge relating to the Flood and the ark is not necessarily indicative that such knowledge was never in their possession. It merely means that if such information existed it was probably obliterated during the massacres.

A rumor began to circulate during the early months of 1970 and eventually reached the ears of the ark-searching groups—a rumor pertaining to a reported reconstruction of the ark which supposedly had been carried out by the hierarchy of the Armenian church about A.D. 300. It was reported that a German Ararat expedition had visited the mountain in 1908, and word leaked out that this group had found actual pieces of wood and iron presumably dating back to A.D. 300. This was supposed to have been part of the ark's reconstruction. Professor Sayim Erin of Istanbul University was said to have been the official scribe for the expedition, and it was suggested that his narrative of the discovery is contained in an 800-page manuscript describing the expedition's activities and filed somewhere in the university library. A thorough search, however, failed to produce the manuscript, and the expedition itself was lost at sea on its return voyage to Germany.

As in the case with most rumors, this, too, was a difficult one to trace. One point, however, projected itself continuously to the foreground in every version; the report that the patriarch of the Armenian church in Jerusalem had a written copy of the official history of the A.D. 300 project in his possession.

A thorough investigation at the University of Istanbul brought no further light to this tale, and so it remained for an on-the-spot exploration in the patriarch's library to relegate the story officially to the file of unsolved mysteries.

Assisted by Sahag Kaleidjan, librarian of the Gulbenkian Library, and Assadour Antreassian, an Armenian writer attached to the Jerusalem Armenian Convent in a semi-official capacity, I spent several days delving into the library's manuscripts.

The bishop in charge of the patriarch's library was the first to voice a note of pessimism. Seated behind a plain mahogany desk, the white-beared old monk listened attentively while I explained to him the reasons for my search. With his hands folded on the lap of his long black robe, he let his eyes roam past the thousands of parchment volumes lining the walls of his inner sanctum while calmly waiting for me to finish my presentation.

"There's no truth to this rumor at all!" he answered, after I had concluded and requested his opinion and cooperation.

"Armenia has always been a rumor mill for pseudo-Christian traditions," he continued. "But knowing the patriarch's library as

I do, I can assure you there is nothing to suggest that there has been a reconstruction of the ark. I can recall only one instance in our history where there has been actual physical contact with a piece of wood from the ancient ark, and that was when Bishop Jacob of Mitspin tried to climb the mountain." He turned in his chair and carefully took an ancient parchment volume from an adjoining desk and opened it.

"In this book, *Ararat,* published in the Armenian Monastery of St. Lazarre in A.D. 1890, it relates the following tradition:

"At this time, the great Bishop of Mitspin, this admirable old man, undefeatable in good works, in truth, this chosen of God, Jacob by name, Persian by origin, left his home directing himself to the mountain in Armenia, that is to say, toward the mountain of Ararat in the territory of the Armenian principality. He was a man filled with the grace of Christ, and one who possessed the power to do miracles." Pausing for a brief moment, he continued his story by combining with it material from other historical reports he had quickly arranged on the desk before him.

"For many years," he quoted, "Jacob had been consumed with the intense desire to find and touch the ancient ark so that he would be able to speak about it with the experience of having touched it, not simply by faith. Having gone to the mountain with a group of fellow travelers, he became extremely fatigued; and, deeply exhausted, he lay down at the foot of the mountain praying for strength and endurance.

"While praying, begging God to show him the ark, a soft and melodious voice interrupted his fervent appeal.

" 'Jacob, do you hear me,' the voice called out. 'Jacob! Jacob!'

" 'I am here, Lord,' the startled bishop of Mitspin answered.

" 'God has heard your prayers and answered your demands,' the voice assured, 'and has given me the task of presenting you with this piece of wood. Now you can return to your flock and cease searching for the ark.'

" 'I looked about me,' Bishop Jacob is quoted as saying, 'and only inches from my head I saw a piece of wood which showed clear evidence of having been cut with an ax from a very big beam of wood.' "

Archbishop Malacia of the Armenian church adds to the story in his *History of the Armenian Church and Nation* by saying that Bishop Jacob thereupon took the wood and brought it to the holy see of Eztmiatzin, which was the seat of the supreme patriarch of the Armenian church.

This story, woven around Bishop Jacob of Mitspin (A.D. 400) has become the basis for many ark tales down through the ages.

The very fact that an Armenian bishop, an official member of the church's hierarchy, found it necessary to make an attempt to locate Noah's ark sometime during the first century of the existence of the Armenian church is in itself an indication that no reconstruction of the ark by the Armenians had taken place. For if the ark had been rebuilt, not only would the location of the original artifact have been known to the Armenian church, but many of its people—most of all its bishops—would have visited the spot to meditate or perhaps to repair the ark or possibly to take its measurements needed for reconstruction at a lower elevation.

But while the Armenian church does not seem to possess exact information regarding the location of the ark itself, it does have definite traditions dealing with the village of Agouri, a settlement on the slopes of Mount Ararat.

It is said that Agouri is the spot where Noah planted the first vineyards. Sahag Kaleidjan, librarian of the Gulbenkian Library, commented that he grew up with the knowledge that Agouri is a place worthy of special attention and veneration. He told me, "It was built on hallowed ground and became the starting point of all post-Deluge civilizations."

He also subscribes to the church-held tradition that the sanctuary of Agouri is built on the site where Noah erected his altar of burnt offering after disembarking from the ark.

Further research in the patriarch's library and the Gulbenkian Library, however, did not yield any more meaningful clues or traditions that could be helpful in our investigation.

Information of an entirely different nature, yet equally as revealing as the legends and traditions of the Flood, has been thus far hidden in the genealogies of the antediluvian patriarchs, found in the book of Genesis. This chapter has been the target of critics, perhaps more than any other book in the Bible. And understandably so, for it contains among others the amazing fact that these patriarchs, ten in all, enjoyed life-spans so drastically different from ours that this chapter has often been relegated to the realm of mythology instead of history. The oldest man listed is Methuselah, having lived 969 years, while Enoch lived only 365. "And he was not," Genesis 5:24 says, "for God took him."

Critics are prepared to discredit this entire chapter, for they say longevity of this type is impossible. If the longevity of our grandparents were the same as that recorded for the patriarchs they would have lived in the time of Christ and would have been able to tell us the story of the crucifixion and of the early spread of Christianity from first-hand experience.

Why are the ages of the antediluvian patriarchs so vital to the story of the Flood? The answer is relatively simple. It enables us to approximate the time of the Flood by figuring forward from the time of creation and backward through Biblical chronology and Jewish history.

It is safe to assume that not only Noah but also his sons, Shem, Ham, and Japheth, as well as their wives and children, carried with them across the water historical facts preserved by them for future generations. That these facts include a list of antediluvian rulers (patriarchs) is to be expected.

In the course of time these names, much like the Flood history itself, have undergone modifications—in many cases complete name changes—to fit the new languages that developed in various parts of the world.

Also, depending on the value these emerging nations placed on social status and leadership qualifications, the patriarchs may have been elevated either to kings or gods. If this is an acceptable assumption, then somewhere among the ancients there must be other lists of ten "patriarchs," and we don't have to look far. Both Babylonian and Egyptian historians have furnished us with lists of ten "antediluvian" kings:*

BIBLICAL PATRIARCHS	*EGYPTIAN GODS*	*CHALDEAN KINGS*
Adam	Ptah	Alorus
Seth	Ra	Aloparus
Enos	Su	Almelon
Cainan	Seb	Ammenon
Mahalaleel	Osirus	Amegalarus
Jared	Set	Daonus
Enoch	Hor	Aedorachus
Methuselah	Tut	Amempsinus
Lamech	Ma	Otiartes
Noah	Hor	Xisuthros

Chaldean and the Biblical accounts of these ancient greats list either their ages, as in the case of the patriarchs; or the length of the king's reign, as in the case of the Chaldeans. From the outset, however, it appears that something must be wrong with the Babylonian account as it credits one of the kings, for example, with a rule of 64,800 years, while another reigned 36,000 years.

Berosus, the Chaldean historian, has a partial answer for us. He claims that the *sarus* is a Babylonian unit of measurement used for chronological purposes—yet he does not give the exact

*From George Smith, *The Chaldean Account of Genesis,* Vol. 6, p. 290; printed in Alfred Rehwinkel, *The Flood,* page 166.

length of the *sarus.* The historian Suidas explains that the Babylonians had not one but *two* different values credited to the *sarus;* one, the civil, corresponding to a time period of 18½ years, the other, the astrological value corresponding to 3,600 years.

It is here that the difference has apparently crept in.

Taking the various ages of the Chaldean antediluvian kings and dividing them by the astrological standard of 3,600 to get to the basic numbers, then multiplying them again with the civil *sarus* standard of 18½ years, the reign of 64,800 years, for example, suddenly becomes 333 years—much more in line with reality. The changes brought about through this method are so startling that in some cases the so-called reigns of the legendary Chaldean kings become almost identical with the important highlights in the lives of the Biblical patriarchs; that is, the birth of their oldest sons.

More important, however, is that this new approach boils down the total reign of the ten antediluvian kings to 2,221 years instead of the hundreds of thousands of years mythology ascribes to them—and this brings the new Chaldean figures of pre-Flood years believably close to the approximate number of years the Bible ascribes to the time that expired between Creation and the Flood.

Due to the fact that Hebrew figures present some very peculiar translation problems creating a number of minor deviations in the numerous Bible translations, the Biblical time span that lapsed between Creation and Deluge is given in at least three different figures.

The Samaritan version of the early Bible books gives a total of 1,307 years before the Flood. The Masoretic text, on which the King James Old Testament is based gives a total of 1,656 years. The Septuagint version gives a total of 2,242 years.

Compare the Septuagint total with the Chaldean account of 2,221 years, and we arrive at a difference of 21 years—a breath of years that is almost negligible.

REFERENCES

1. From the private files of Aaron Smith.
2. Based on research by Fernand Navarra, Ararat explorer and author of *Jai Trouve L'Arche.*
3. Johannes Riem, *Die Sintfult in Sage und Wissenschaft,* page 7.
4. Hugh Miller, *The Testimony of the Rocks,* page 284.
5. From the private files of Aaron Smith.
6. Lowell Thomas, *Hungry Waters—The Story of the Great Flood,* page 184.
7. J. S. Bartlett, *History of Wyoming,* Vol. 1, p. 62.
8. *Mythology of All Races,* X, page 222.
9. Rehwinkel, *op. cit.,* p. 128.

CHAPTER 3

While searching for evidences of the Deluge tragedy, I have often imagined myself standing among the fierce antediluvians, watching with growing astonishment ole' man Noah build a ship. Many times I have imagined listening to the shouts of ridicule, the echoing chorus of sneering laughter, and the barrage of discouraging remarks aimed at Noah and his sons while they labored on the ark for over one hundred years.

They must have been the "big laugh" of the century, the object of innumerable jokes. Just to see Noah sweat and preach, never ceasing but always working toward that great day ahead. If TV had existed in those days, Noah most certainly would have pulled a top rating.

I have often tried to "feel" the fright and bewilderment of Noah's contemporaries as they watched hundreds of land animals wend their way toward the ark, two by two, as if driven by an unseen force, and then the final closing of the door after Noah and his family entered the ship before the onlooking crowd. But the growing terror of the spectators must have been unequaled as suddenly torrential rains fell on them, while devastating waterspouts filled the valleys. Swept on by terrifying storms and earthquakes, the flooding soon took on cataclysmic proportions. One after another the people fled to higher ground, leaving homes, deserting cities, reaching for safety only to be pulled under by the force of the onrushing waters.

Outside the ark man ceased to exist; flying reptiles were no more; great dinosaurs perished from the face of the earth. Plant life, once so abundant, was destroyed in the profusion of water. These factors taken together create a mystery which baffles scientists today. The suddenness of it all even now puzzles the best minds in paleontology, for in the place of this wealth of fauna and flora, the earth's crust is now filled with myriads of early life remains embedded in the sprawling rock formations of the postdiluvial earth.

The unprecedented disappearance of many kinds of plants and animals and of entire civilizations must have left traces discernible to the investigative mind. We assume that the pre-Flood world was well-developed, with its animal and human population numbering in the millions and spread around the globe.

The traces *are* there—some of the answers, at least, lie buried in the rocks.

Much like our great storms of today, the Genesis Flood was no doubt accompanied by violent winds that swept the turbulent waters first to the lower levels of the land masses, then continued upward until the peaks of the highest mountains were completely inundated. Their force and magnitude not only covered the globe, but the effects were so far-reaching and monstrous in their scope that it made the earth tremble. It was a catastrophe of dimensions that has never before and never since occurred in the history of this planet. The upheaval caused by this tragedy was so total that today many of the great mountains of the earth, whether they be the Rockies, the Andes, the Himalayas, or the Alps, bear the scars. Many contain seashells and others signs of ocean life that existed thousands of years ago. True, human history is old—or so we claim—but the silent voice of the rocks predates the Egyptian and Babylonian records by many a year. Deluge geologists place the age difference within the range of a few thousand years; evolutionists squeeze in an extra few hundred million.

A global flood of such proportions as this one certainly must have deposited tremendous amounts of sedimentation on the bottoms of the newly formed water masses. Thus, inasmuch as the Flood has been described as a *universal one,* it should be possible to find evidences of at least remnants of such deposits; and this is exactly the case. *It has been scientifically estimated that over 75 percent of the earth's surface is sedimentary in nature,* some areas revealing more sediment than others. The United States has immense sedimentary areas located in inland California, the Colorado plateau, and the Midwest plains; but India, to date, has presented us with the deepest sedimentary basin known to man —all of 60,000 feet deep!

Evolutionists advocate a pet theory that presumably accounts for this sedimentary layer. "Caused by slow erosion followed by slow accumulation over the years," is their explanation. But does this sound reasonable or even probable?

"Such processes as gradual submergence and the slow accumulation of sediments by erosion," writes Dr. H. G. Coffin in *Creation,* "seems inadequate to account for the great quantities of water- and wind-deposited materials. Adjacent areas do not provide sufficient material for deposition on such a scale. But a flood of sufficient extent to cover all land, and a storm of great violence that stirred roiled water or soft mud is sufficient to account for the transport of vast amounts of sedimentary material over great distances, and the filling in of depressions irrespective of the height or extent of adjacent landscapes."[1]

Scientists generally agree that if there are "exceptions" to their claim of gradual deposits, the sedimentary deposits of the northern Rockies must be ranked among them. For there, well preserved water ripple marks and a countless number of fossilized trilobites, together with other delicate fossils surviving without a sign of disintegration, are among the features that suggest that they were not laid to rest in a slow and gentle manner, but abruptly and suddenly as if by a great and unexpected catastrophe.

The "voice of the rocks" speaks forcefully. Many reputable museums have at least a number of prehistoric animals on exhibit. Dinosaurs and flying reptiles have their place in history books, and we have grown up aware of some of the basic facts concerning the giant creatures of our distant past. The meaning of the tiny fossil shells, fish, and small vertebrates found in the rocks are not so well-known, yet their "voice" often speaks louder.

In discussing the presence of fish in sedimentary rock, Immanuel Velikovsky writes: "When a fish dies, its body floats on the surface or sinks to the bottom and is devoured rather quickly, actually in a matter of hours, by other fish. However, the fossil fish found in sedimentary rock is very often preserved with all its bones intact. Entire shoals of fish over large areas, numbering billions of specimens, are found in a state of agony, but with no mark of a scavenger's attack."[2]

Many scientists' findings bear this out. Robert Broom, the well-known South African paleontologist, has estimated that in the Karroo formation alone eight hundred thousand million skeletons of vertebrate animals can be found.

Describing the Devonian rocks which cover most of England, geologist H. Miller writes: "At this period in our history, some terrible catastrophe involved in sudden destruction the fish of an area at least a hundred miles from boundary to boundary, perhaps much more. The same platform in Orkney as at Cromarty is strewed thick with remains, which exhibit unequivocally the marks of violent death. The figures are contorted, contracted, curved; the tail in many instances bent around the head; the spines stick out; the fins are spread to the full as in fish that die in convulsions."[3] The area described by Miller covers approximately 10,000 square miles and has all the distinguishing marks of having undergone the effects of a destructive force.

There are also petrified "fish beds" of enormous proportions even closer to home. Concerning beds of herring fossils found in the Miocene shales of California, Harry S. Ladd of the United States Geological Survey writes: "More than a billion fish, averaging 6 to 8 inches in length, died on 4 square miles of bay bottom."[4]

Various reports in my files speak of a find in the Geisental lignite deposits in Germany. It appears that in this one location a mixture of plants, animals, and even insects from all climatic areas of the world are buried in one common "mass grave."

Describing the discovery in detail, Wilfred Frances observed that "in some cases leaves have been deposited and preserved in a fresh condition, the chlorophyl being still green, so that the 'green layer' is used as a marker during excavations. Among the insects present are beautifully colored tropical beetles, with soft parts of the body, including the contents of the intestines, preserved intact. Normally such materials decay or change in color within a few hours of death, so that preservation by inclusion in an aseptic medium must have been sudden and complete."[5]

Speaking of dinosaurs, Edwin H. Colbert says: "The great extinction that wiped out *all* of the dinosaurs, large and small, in all parts of the world, and at the same time, brought to an end various lines of reptilian evolution, was one of the outstanding events in the history of life and in the history of the earth. . . . It was an event that has defied all attempts at a satisfactory explanation."[6]

Even George Gaylord Simpson, one of the most respected men in paleontology, is baffled when confronted with this problem. He admits: "It is as if the curtain were rung down suddenly on a stage where all the leading roles were taken by reptiles, especially dinosaurs, in great number and in bewildering variety, and rose again immediately to reveal the same setting but an entirely new cast in which the dinosaurs do not appear at all, other reptiles are mere super-numeraries and the leading parts are all played by mammals."[7]

But more! The same crisis in the history of mother earth that destroyed the dinosaurs and the other animals also destroyed the great marine reptiles—the plesiosaurs, the mosasaurs, and the ichthyosaurs. Even though they lived in the sea, they could not escape the fate that befell their land-bound brothers. And the air, too, made its sacrifice. Where are the great winged dragons, the pterosaurs with their wingspan of twenty-five feet? Only fossil remains can tell us about them, for they also disappeared from the scene of life. They shared the same fate.

It must have been a worldwide catastrophe to hit all these great beasts at the same time. We find their remains in nearly every continent. Some geologists are willing to go that far in their reasoning. Many others shy away from it. Recently I encountered a statement that leans toward the "Great Single Catastrophe."

L. Sprague de Camp and Catherine Crook de Camp write concerning this in *The Day of the Dinosaur,* pages 22, 201: "So far no logical way has been found to connect the known cause of the extinction of individual species with these worldwide Great Deaths. Some other cause, operating on a worldwide basis would seem to be called for."

It was only a matter of time before a few researchers began to dream about trying to equal the rapid burial process scientifically, or if that were not feasible, then to attempt a duplication of the quick preservation of the delicate structures of the smallest of these animals through natural processes.

Zangerl and Richardson tried. Coffin describes their efforts as follows: "In attempting to evaluate the rate of fossilization in the Pennsylvania black shales of Indiana, they placed dead fish in the protecting wire cages and dropped them into the black muds at the bottom of several Louisiana lagoons or bayous. These black muds are thought to resemble the sediments from which the dark shales were derived. To the great surprise of the investigators, fish weighing from one half to three fourths pound were found to have all the soft parts reduced and all the bones completely disarticulated in six and one-half days! Decomposition to the state of total disarticulation apparently occurs at great speed, perhaps in less time than indicated above, since none were checked before six and one-half days. Delicate fossil fish showing every minute ray and bone in position are common and must represent a burial by oxygen- and bacteria-excluding sediments within hours of death if this experiment is a valid indication."[8]

A burial by a sudden deluge is again the only reasonable conclusion. Hours has to be the answer; not six and one half days!

Due to our civilization's ever-increasing demand for fuel, the world's deposits of coal and oil supplies are rapidly diminishing. But strange and wonderful finds have emerged through the study of the earth's coal deposits; facts which again strengthen the concept of the worldwide Flood.

Dr. Harold Coffin, of the Geoscience Research Institute, Berrien Springs, Michigan, has done extensive research into the background of the coal beds and has uncovered some interesting facts. Writing about minable coal seams, he says, "The thickness of peat needed to produce one foot of coal depends on the number of factors such as the type of peat, the amount of water in the vegetable matter, and the type of coal. The scientific literature on coal gives figures ranging from a few feet to as many as twenty. Let us assume that ten feet would near the average figure. On this basis, a coal seam thirty feet thick would require the compression of *300 feet of peat.* A 400-foot seam of coal would be the result of a *fantastic 4,000 feet of peat.* . . . There are few peat bogs, marshes, or swamps anywhere in the world today that reach 100 feet. Most of them are less than 50 feet. A much more reasonable alternative theory is that the vegetable matter has been concentrated and collected into an area by some force, undoubtedly water. . . .

"The concept of a global deluge that eroded out the forests and plant cover of the pre-Flood world, collected it in great mats of drifting debris, and eventually dropped it on the emerging land or on the sea bottom is the most reasonable answer to this problem of the great extent and uniform thickness of coal beds."[9] (Italics supplied.)

It has never been easy to arrive at a possible date for the "Great Catastrophe," yet some archaeologists have made various educated guesses, based on the latest criteria used in their respective fields.

Regarding the birth of the Egyptian civilization, H. R. Hall, the Egyptologist, states: "We think that the 1st dynasty began not before 3400 and not much later than 3200 B.C. . . . A. Scharff, however would bring the date down to about 3000 B.C.; and it must be admitted that his arguments are good and that at any rate it is more probable that *the date of the 1st Dynasty is later than 3400* B.C. than earlier."[10] (Italics supplied.)

Comments Dr. Samuel Noah Kramer, research professor of Assyriology at the University of Pennsylvania concerning the Sumerians: "The dates of Sumer's early history have always been surrounded with uncertainty, and they have not been satisfactorily settled by tests with the new method of radiocarbon dating. . . . Be that as it may be, it seems that the *people called Sumerians did not arrive in the region until nearly 3000* B.C."[11] (Italics supplied.)

The Chinese civilization, too, has been subjected to an educated estimate; for according to Ralph Lindon, the anthropologist, "the earliest Chinese date which can be assigned with any probability is 2250 B.C., based on an astronomical reference in the *Book of History*."[12]

Traditional Bible chronology gives us the year 2448 B.C. as an estimate for the occurrence of the Flood. Since the dates proposed by the scholars, as given above, are only approximate figures, we may conclude that they can be accommodated to the same event—that of a world destroyed by water; more so, since the average of their dates (3,000, 3,000, 2,250, 2,740, and 2,620) gives us

2723 B.C. as the target date. But there's more. In late 1960, during the aftermath of one of the most interesting ark expeditions of recent years, a team member, Dr. Arthur J. Brandenberger, professor of photogrammetry at Ohio State University, received a letter from Mr. George F. Dodwell, retired government astronomer of south Australia and director of the Adelaide Observatory.

Writing in regard to the recent expedition to Turkey, Dodwell stated: "I am especially interested in such a remarkable result, because I have been making during the last 26 years an extensive investigation of what we know in astronomy as the secular variation of the obliquity of the ecliptic, and from a study of the available ancient observations of the position of the sun at the solstices during the last three thousand years, I find a curve which, after allowing for all known changes, [shows] a typical exponential curve of recovery of the earth's axis after a sudden change from a former nearly vertical position to an inclination of 26½ degrees, from which it was returned to an equilibrium at the present inclination of 23½ degrees during the interval of the succeeding 3,194 years to A.D. 1850.

"The date of the change in the earth's axis, 2345 B.C.," he continued, "is none other than that of the flood recorded in the Bible, and the resulting conclusion is that the Biblical account of the flood as a universal one, together with its story of Noah's Ark, is historically true."

Early in my research, I became quite involved with the problem of trying to determine the distribution of the human race prior to the time of the Flood. A popular assumption was—and in many instances still is—that the pre-Flood world was sparsely populated and that for reasons of survival and mutual aid, the population had not as yet spread beyond the Mesopotamia area. No one knows, of course, with any degree of certainty what the population of the earth may have been in Noah's time; but this does not mean that a careful speculation concerning the number of humanity at that time is not in order. In my quest for facts, I encountered scientists who were convinced that civilization had not spread farther than the Tigris-Euphrates region of the Middle East. Such is the case of my old mentor, Professor Dr. J. H. Hospers, of the University of Groningen in the Netherlands, who also held the view that the Deluge was "only" a local affair and of no real importance to the world beyond Mesopotamia. None of these experts, however, has examined the historical reports, flood legends, and traditions which indicate that the Flood was a universal and not merely a local one.

Humanity was still in its infant stages, they add, and was still emotionally bound to its cradle, the Middle East. The reason the survivors of the Flood claim it was universal, they continue, is that to *them* it seemed as if the whole world was being swallowed up by water. They were not aware of the great world beyond that surrounded their small Middle Eastern home, and consequently they regarded it as a global flood.

As simple as this theory may appear, it does not explain the wide distribution of the Flood traditions, nor the geological facts that indicate a global deluge, nor the archaeological evidence pointing toward a total catastrophe. But a civilization completely devastated by angry waves does not relate a story, except a silent one; and even the billions of animals that were annihilated by the turbulent waters are of little help.

Only a scrutinizing examination of the Biblical story of events surrounding the Flood and findings of modern biologists and authorities on population growth can provide us with the explanation.

The fifth chapter of Genesis points out some very revealing statistics concerning the ages of the antediluvian race. Adam, according to this chapter lived 930 years; Seth 912 years; Enos 905; Cainan 910; Mahalaleel 895; Jared 962; Methuselah 969; Lamech 777, and Noah a healthy 950 years. The average of these being 923 years.

There are many diverse factors which can account for their fantastic life-span. Originally man was undoubtedly endowed with much more vitality in order to survive the birth pangs of civilization and the struggles for physical survival, and sufficient indications lead us to believe that the pre-Flood world had a more agreeable climate, where tropical and subtropical plants flourished in areas that are now deserts and ice fields. Plants grew on virgin soil.

Today, with our polluted human race, an increase of five children per family is considered average if measured on a world-wide basis, taking into account that the reproductive capacity of the average woman is limited to approximately thirty or thirty-five years of her natural lifespan. Families with eight, ten, or more children were certainly common not so long ago, and even today large families are still the accepted norm in many countries. Therefore, if for the average human life-span of our day the fertility period is only 30 to 35 years, how much longer must it have been in the days when the antediluvian population enjoyed life-spans reaching 900 years or more?

To those critics who feel 900 years is a bit much to accept, Dr. Hans Selye, Director of the Institute of Experimental Surgery, Montreal University, replies as follows: "Medicine has assembled a fund of knowledge that will now serve, I believe, as a point of departure for studying the causes of old age. If the causes of aging can be found, there is no good medical reason to believe that it will not be possible for science to find some practical way of slowing the process down, or even bringing it to a standstill."[13]

What a reversal of the aging process would mean to our already overpopulated world is something I will gladly leave in the hands of the psychiatrists and sociologists.

Assuming that the reproductive capacity of the antediluvian mother was equal to half her age (again taking today's reproductive capacity versus life-span as a basis), then we arrive at the startling conclusion that 400 years of reproductive capacity per woman would not be unusual. It is here that we must begin our calculations.

Allowing an antediluvian mother excessive reproductive capacities, a family of eighteen to twenty children does not seem unreasonable. By accepting the genealogy mentioned in the book of Genesis, and agreeing that between Adam and Noah there were ten generations, we arrive at the following possible population estimate for the antediluvian world:*

First generation	2
Second generation	18
Third generation	162
Fourth generation	1,458
Fifth generation	13,133
Sixth generation	118,098
Seventh generation	1,062,882
Eighth generation	9,565,938
Ninth generation	86,093,442
Tenth generation	774,840,979

Almost seven-hundred-and-seventy-five million people! Add to these the surviving members of previous generations, and the number may have been close to 900,000,000, a figure similar to the world's population of about 150 years ago. If we were to assume that families of the antediluvian world had an average of twenty children, then the figure of 775,000,000 increases to 2,000,000,000 not counting the surviving members of previous generations!

A report circulated in 1959 gave credence indirectly to the possibility of a large antediluvian population.

"During the first half of the 19th century," it states, "world population reached 1 billion; in 1930 the figure was about 2 billion. In 1957 and 1958 alone the earth's population increased by 90 million, a figure twice the population of France, and the

*From Alfred Rehwinkel, *The Flood*.

world is expected to have 3 billion inhabitants by 1962. The acceleration of population growth in underdeveloped countries is especially spectacular. Annual increases of 2 percent or more are usual in most of these countries, and in some there is a growth of 3 percent."[14]

World population now approximates 3,800,000,000, and will soon reach the 4,000,000,000 figure. Thus it is possible, assuming a high birth rate and low death rate, that the antediluvian world was populated by a race that covered the face of the globe.

But then the Flood came and everything changed.

How far-reaching the effects of the Flood must have been on the survivors of the human race is illustrated in a graph prepared by William R. Vis, showing the contrast between the ante- and postdiluvian patriarchs. "A study of this chart," he explains, "shows in a striking way that something *extremely significant* happened to the earth and to man at the time of the flood. It would seem that whatever this was, it probably removed the dominant factor for the long life of the patriarchs. . . . The scientific explanation is not evident. Could some antediluvian climatic or other condition have been extremely favorable for long life in man? Perhaps future scientific research will cast some light on this." (Italics supplied.)

The decrease in life-span, coupled to the vivid memory of the terrible destruction still visible on the face of the earth now, almost 5,000 years after the Deluge, has given rise to many traditions and legends. Noah's sons and their families were perhaps responsible for many of these Flood legends in existence, for even though they were all subjected to the same terrifying experience, each left the ark with his own personal impressions of the tragedy. Each man's background colored his private recollection, and the minute changes in each story developed, with the passing of time, into major differences as the versions stayed alive through successive generations, being told and retold from father to son. And when they moved outward, searching for new boundaries beyond the mountains of Ararat, the Flood story went with them and laid the groundwork for the mythology concerning the Flood.

A few years back, during preparation for the 1970 expedition, a listener attending one of the lectures concerning the proposed expedition approached me afterwards and commented cynically, "I'll believe all you've said if you can prove to me that the legendary ark was really big enough to hold all of the representatives of the animal kingdom at the time of the Flood!" With this question he opened up an entirely different area of ark research, for calculating the dimension of the ark is one of the most difficult problems in the entire story.

Why?

It is because a very basic element, the cubit, the unit of measurement according to which the Bible describes the dimensions, has become a matter of speculation down through the ages. Webster (Third New International) calls it "any of various ancient units of length based on the length of the forearm from the elbow to the tip of the middle finger and usu. equal to about 18 inches but sometimes to 21 or more." However, if we cannot prove the size of the antediluvian man and his forearm, we cannot reach a fixed conclusion as to the antediluvian cubit.

Estimates vary on the possible dimensions of the antediluvian man. Some speculate that he may have reached twelve feet in height, with an average weight of more than 1,200 pounds. If this is true, then more fuel is added to the controversy. In centuries past the distance between the ruling king's elbow and fingertips determined the length of the cubit. Can you imagine how complex the problem becomes in attempting to arrive at an accurate dimension for this basic ancient measurement? The Webster estimate may be a good approximation, but if the human ulna in a pre-Flood man measured 28 inches, and we add 9 inches for the hand (based on ⅓ of the length of the forearm), this brings us to a total of 37 inches, or approximately *twice* that of the most conservative estimate of today!

While studying the dimensions furnished by the Bible, Charles A. Totten, professor of military science and tactics at Yale University, has compiled some relevant figures. He writes "The dimensions of the ark are given in the Bible as 300 cubits long, fifty cubits wide and thirty cubits high. It had three decks. Regarding the cubit as eighteen inches, the floor space on one deck would be 33,750 square feet. On the three decks of the ark there was then a total of 101,250 square feet of deck space. But since it was likely that the small and medium-sized animals were put in cages, in tiers, one above the other, not only the floor space but the cubic space must be considered. The cubic capacity of the ark at 18 inches as the measure of the cubit, was for each deck 500,000 cubic feet, or 1,500,000 feet for the three decks.

"However, as we have seen, it is not at all certain that the cubit of the ark was eighteen inches. There was never any definite length of the cubit in ancient days. Different cubits existed. Most common was the cubit of the elbow, that is, the distance from the elbow to the fingertip. There was also the cubit of the arm pit or the distance of the whole arm. Naturally these lengths vary with the size of the person measured. The cubit also varied from country to country. Ancient Egypt had two lengths for it at different times. One was the length of a newborn child; the other was the length of the king at a certain age. We may say that a cubit of 20.7 inches was about the standard measure of the Egyptian and also of the Assyrian, Chaldean, and Babylonian empires. Moses was directed to work according to a pattern shown him. The so-called 'great-cubit' of Ezekiel revealed to him by God was an ordinary cubit plus a hand's breadth, or about two feet.

"Supposing this to have been the length of the cubit, the ark was then 600 feet long, and 100 feet wide and sixty feet high, having a capacity of 3,600,000 feet."[15]

What does all this mean in comparison to modern ocean liners, for example? What may have been the freight-carrying capacity of the ark compared to modern cargo transport methods?

LENGTH OF ARK BASED ON VARIOUS CUBIT SIZES

TYPE AND LENGTH OF CUBIT	DIMENSIONS OF ARK	CUBIT FEET CAPACITY	BOX CAR CAPACITY	COMPARABLE TO OCEAN LINER
Common Hebrew cubit ranged from 17½ to 18 inches Based on 18 in/p/cubit	450x75x45 ft.	1,518,750 gross tonnage 15,187	421	Renaissance, (French) 12,000 tons 492 feet
Babylonian/Assyrian Chaldean cubit 20 inches per cubit	600x100x60 ft.	3,600,000 gross tonnage 36,000	1,000	Gripsholm, (Swed) 631 feet 23,215 tons
Antediluvian estimate 36 inches per cubit	900x150x90 ft.	12,150,000 gross tonnage 121,500	3,375	Queen Elizabeth II 963 feet 65,863 tons

Difference in tonnage between ark and ships of comparable length is accounted for by the rectangular shape of the ark allowing for maximum and available space.

Searching for an object is generally facilitated once its size has been established. Granted, in looking for an ark having tremendous proportions, a few feet more or less aren't that important. However, the various cubit calculations lead to dimensions so varied that a comparison should be considered.

Was the ark really equal to the tremendous task that has been ascribed to it? Let's take a look at the accompanying chart. The dimensions are staggering, and even more so when one realizes the full meaning of the boxcar capacity listed in the chart. If we figure that the average capacity per boxcar can be set at 67 animals, then the total number of animals able to have been stored in the ark of that approximate size, utilizing only 75 percent of the available space, would be: (a) 28,207 animals for the

"18-inch cubit ark," (b) 67,000 for the "20-inch cubit ark," (c) 226,125 animals for the "antediluvian-estimate ark," and this would still leave adequate space for supplies and living quarters for Noah's family!

While studying these figures, even the most ardent critic can certainly have no doubt as to the fact that the capacity of the ship was adequate for the task. What type of animals actually boarded the ark and whether the species of the antediluvian age were the same as we encounter today are questions that have never really entered the realm of ark research. This is because they would be too closely associated with the biological and the supernatural aspects of the Deluge and would have no bearing on the search for the true artifact. Also beyond the scope of ark research is the question as to how Noah was able to construct this formidable ship in the 120 years allotted to him. Inquiry into this has been done by George McCready Price, Alfred Rehwinkel, Henry M. Morris, Arthur C. Custance, and others. But we are interested mainly in the extent of the Flood, the size of the ark, and the possible location of its remains. Efforts of the ark groups since 1946 have been directed at finding answers to these three questions.

Closely related to the capacity of the ark is its design. By combining the various historical descriptions, some "ark-eologists" have arrived at what they felt was the general design of the ship. This has been important in evaluating the diversity of eyewitness accounts made by people claiming to have seen the ark, especially within the last 150 years. Inasmuch as it would be a general shelter, designed to *float*, not to *sail*, it would be reasonable to assume that it may have had the shape of a flat-bottomed box.

During my early years of studying this subject, while I attended the University of Groningen in the Netherlands, I came across a manuscript mentioning a Dutch merchant named Pieter Jansen. In the beginning of the seventeenth century, he commissioned a shipyard to build a scale model of the ark according to the measurements given in the book of Genesis. His scale model is reported to have been 120 feet long, twenty feet wide, and twelve feet high. It proved not only more seaworthy than contemporary vessels, but its gross tonnage was one-third larger than ships built to more modern designs. The Frenchman Fernand Navarra, who climbed Mount Ararat several times during the post-war period, and whose contribution to the search for the ark will be discussed in a later chapter, built a small scale model based on available information. His rectangular model, which he feels is as accurate a replica of the ark as can be constructed, is not necessarily drastically different from most imaginary arks, but it does furnish a visual presentation of the possible shape and design.

The Babylonian/Assyrian deluge account also gave the ship a rather flat description. In lines 57 through 61, the Gilgamesh Epic states that its floor space was one "iku," a measurement which has been translated to mean 3,600 square meters or approximately one acre. It reads, "One iku was its floor space, one hundred and twenty cubits each was the height of its walls; one hundred twenty cubits measured each side of its deck." The record continues by stating that the ark was built with six lower decks, dividing it into seven stories. This leads to only one conclusion—the boat in which Utnapishti escaped was an exact cube! It is doubtful that this was the actual shape of the historical ark, as the distribution of its heavy cargo extending all the way to the seventh floor would have made it extremely vulnerable to capsizing in the storms that surely accompanied the Deluge.

There are other possible interpretations, the oldest being Origen's description of the ark in "Homilies on Genesis." In it he says, "Judging from the description, I imagine that it had a rectangular bottom and that the walls converged gradually as they rose to the top, where the width was only one cubit."

Origen continued: "Given the conditions resulting from the rain and the Deluge, a more appropriate shape could not have been given to the ark than this narrow summit which let the rainwater run down, like a roof, and this rectangular bottom flat on the water, keeping the ark from pitching or sinking under the action of the wind and the waves or because of the animals' restlessness."

But what about the specifications? you may wonder. Why this specific ratio? Why not, for example, 300 by 200 by 20, or some other ratio?

The specifications as mentioned in Genesis speak of a boxlike construction, but not a *square* box. Not so in the Gilgamesh Epic, where the ark was but a crudely designed cubic vessel having the tendency to keep turning with each gust of wind as if caught in a gigantic whirlpool.

Noah's ark was different however. Its ratio of six to one (300 cubits by 50) has tremendous advantages over the cubic contraption of the Babylonian epic. From a point of stability and rolling, the ratio of 6:1 is about as perfect as can be desired. Some of the giant tankers have a ratio of 7:1. The shipbuilder Brunel, in quest for the ultimate in passenger comfort, designed an ocean liner known as the *Great Britain* in 1844. The vessel's dimensions were 522 by 51 by 32½ feet—proportions almost identical with the dimensions of Noah's Ark. But whereas Noah built his ship as the first of its kind, Brunel had several thousand years of shipbuilding expertise to rely on; yet, all the accumulated knowledge could not give him a ratio more perfect than that of the ark.

The last model of the ark built with what was claimed original research made news in early 1968, when Meir Ben Uri, a leading Israeli religious artist and architect displayed his reproduction in Solomon's Palace in Jerusalem, seat of Israel's Chief Rabbinate.

In February, 1968, an article entitled "Making Noah's Ark Credible," appeared in *Christianity Today*. It stated:

"Ben Uri's hobby is reconstructing Old Testament objects as they might have looked in fact—not fancy. He uses descriptions from the Bible, plus calculations from numerical values of the Hebrew words.

"Earlier projects were the seven-branched candlestick and the Ark of the Covenant. Both holy objects, he scoffs, have been over-embellished by Byzantine influences.

"Insisting that 'every letter is correct and makes the Bible a holy source for research,' Ben Uri went to work on Genesis 6:14-16. He rid himself of current architectural ideas and projected his thoughts to an age along the Persian Gulf when bamboo and pitch served as construction materials.

" 'The ark couldn't have been constructed as a tower, a house, or a temple,' he figures, 'but may have been similar in shape to the smaller ark used by Moses' mother to conceal her son on the Nile.'

"In Ben Uri's theory . . . the ark rested on its side with 'the door . . . set in the side thereof' during construction before the flood. Thus entering animals had to walk an incline of no more than thirty degrees. As the water rose, the ark righted itself and floated, raising the door well above the water. The entire top of the ark had continuous skylights for ventilation. Waste from animals flowed down to the lowest point and provided ballast. With waste disposed below, and light and air circulating to all levels, no sanitation problems developed.

"He figured the ark weighed about 6,000 tons, with a load capacity of perhaps three times that weight—easily enough space for the animals, Noah's family, and the food required.

"Ben Uri uses a rhomboid design of two equal triangles joined along their bases. A rectangular shape would have required too many supports, allowing insufficient space for live cargo, he says, and would not have provided the buoyance needed to float such a load.

"The simple, functional design required little more than a number of equal sized triangular templates fitted together, with the necessary internal wooden accommodations. He says that even if Noah was inexperienced he could easily have done such a building job."

For centuries now, Christians have regarded Mount Ararat in eastern Turkey as the resting place of Noah's ark, basing their belief on the Genesis account of the Flood. Many names have been given to the mountain.

The Hebrews call it Urartu; the Persians give it the name of Koh-I-Noe; the Armenians refer to the same mountain as Masis, while today, the Turks call it Agri-Dagh.

Not all archaeologists agree that the mountain we know as Ararat is the same one mentioned in Genesis as the resting place of the ark, even though the Turkish name translated means "Mountain of the Ark" and the Persian name Koh-I-Noe means "Mountain of Noah." It is true that the Babylonian legend has Utnapishti landing his boat on Mount Nisir, and the Moslem world stubbornly believes that the ark landed on Mount Djudi (located farther south). Measured against traditions, however, that have sprung up around Mount Ararat since the beginning of time, the latter view is hardly worth considering, as more and more Islamic scholars have openly admitted that the real Mount Djudi may after all be the mountain known as Ararat.

While roaming about the countryside of Ararat, I was reminded of Noah and his ark wherever I went. Even the "discoverer-at-home," while sitting near the warmth of his own hearth, can find places on the map of Turkey indicative of Noah's landing. Nakhitchevan, a city southeast of Ararat, was still called Apobaterion during the time of Flavius Josephus. Its present name means "the place where Noah landed." Old timers in that city will proudly lead the way to the traditional grave site of Noah. A small town called Aghuri, set on the slope of the mountain, is the time-honored place where Noah is supposed to have planted his first vineyard after disembarking from the ark. Interesting also is the fact that Erivan, capital of Russian Armenia, translates as "place of the first appearance."

At various times throughout recorded history, the names "Armenia" and "Ararat" have been used to describe the same area, and even today the name Ararat refers to the province around the mountain of Ararat, not just the mountain itself. It is perhaps because of the many traditions naming Mount Ararat as the landing place of the ark that the Armenians refer to the mountain as "Mother of the World." It always has been their symbol of unity and has served as focal point of their traditions.

Ararat is a massive mountain, an extinct volcano that dominates the entire Armenian plateau overlooking the Russian, Turkish, and Iranian border area. Thus it is a spot of immense strategic importance. The mountain itself is about twenty-five miles in diameter. Because of its tremendous size, it has presented numerous obstacles to ark searchers in the past.

Seeing Ararat for the first time is an exhilarating experience. Rising high above the Bayazid plateau, Greater Ararat extends its broad-shouldered dome to a height of 16,945 feet, faithfully guarded on the southeastern flank by Little Ararat, the second peak of the mountain, which is separated from Greater Ararat by only seven miles. Reaching to a height of 12,877 feet, Little Ararat is a fitting companion to the big peak in this grand scheme of massive design, for there are no other neighboring peaks to detract from Ararat's majestic grandeur.

Never is the mountain without snow, even though during the hot summer months the snowline may retreat to a height of 14,000 feet. The rest of the year both Greater and Little Ararat are enveloped in a cloak of snow and present a grand view to those who venture into the area.

But a change occurs during July, August, and September when the mountain begins to display its distinct color zones, ranging the distance from the base of the mountain to the towering summit. A grayish volcanic ash covers the lower slopes, making a lasting impression when seen during the spring and fall seasons. Above that level, rising to a height of 11,500 feet, starts the second level known for its good pastures and juniper trees. This zone is a vivid green, and it is here that Kurdish and Armenian shepherds graze their sheep.

Above this is the black zone consisting of basaltic rocks, which underlies the dazzling white dome of everlasting ice and snow. Impressive? It most certainly is! No man who has seen Ararat will ever forget the majestic monolith that rises to a towering height above the plain of Bayazit.

Other than the devastation of the 1840's, no significant changes are known to have occurred in historic times. The immense boulders that careened down the mountain on that fateful day destroyed the town of Aghuri at the foot of the mountain. The quake also greatly enlarged the deep crevass on the side of the mountain known as the Aghuri Gorge. Eyewitnesses to the explosion of July 2, 1840, say the ground was shaken by a series of pulsating shock waves, creating huge fissures on the slopes of the mountain. Stabbing gas flames and flying boulders presented an awesome spectacle. The eight-hundred-year-old Monastery of St. James also fell victim to the blast.

Since that time, Ararat has veiled itself in mysterious quietness. With lofty indifference, it has witnessed the Turkish-Armenian conflicts, and because of a political border agreement with Russia, it is now separated from the geographic remainder of old Armenia. The Russians have recognized the Armenian part of the USSR as a separate republic, Russian Armenia. The Turks, on the other hand, have *not* recognized the yearning for limited independence of the Armenians still living in Turkish Armenia, much to the dislike of the inhabitants of the region. The Russian attitude has eliminated much of the friction that once existed between Armenians and Russians, and the old Armenian Orthodox Church again takes an important position in Soviet Armenia.

Only in recent years has Ararat again come under public scrutiny, but this time not because of political entanglements, but through the renewed interest in the Biblical story of Noah's ark.

REFERENCES

1. Harold G. Coffin, *Creation—Accident or Design?* page 65.
2. I. Velikovsky, *Earth in Upheaval,* page 222.
3. H. Miller, *The Old Red Sandstone,* page 221.
4. Harry S. Ladd, "Ecology, Paleontology and Stratigraphy," *Science,* Vol. 129, Jan. 9, 1959, p. 72.
5. Wilfrid Francis, *Coal, Its Formation and Composition,* page 18.
6. Edwin H. Colbert, *The Age of Reptiles,* page 191.
7. Quoted by Carl Dunbar in *Historical Geology,* page 426.
8. Coffin, *op. cit.,* pp. 73, 74.
9. *Ibid.,* p. 76.
10. H. R. Hall, Article: "Archaeology," *Encyclopedia Britannica* (1959 ed.), Vol. 8, p. 37.
11. S. N. Kramer, "The Sumerians," *Scientific American,* Vol. 197, October, 1957, p. 72.
12. Ralph Linton, *The Tree of Culture* (New York: Alfred A. Knopf Publishing Co., 1955), page 520.
13. Hans Selye, "Is Aging Curable?" *Science Digest,* Vol. 46, December, 1959, p. 1.
14. "Population Growth," *Science,* Vol. 129, April 3, 1959, p. 882.
15. B. C. Nelson, *The Deluge Story in Stone,* page 156.

CHAPTER 4

The intensive search for the elusive ark is supported by many stories, some scientific, others of a more historical nature; still others merely the result of an over-inventive mind. The majority of them, however, are old and often deemed unreliable.

It is no wonder that "ark-eologists" went nearly wild when the first "recent" eyewitness account hit the headlines in the early 1940's.

Finally someone had *seen* the ark!

It was Benjamin F. Allen, a retired lawyer-turned-researcher who acted as the literary catalyst.

For many years Allen had been a staunch advocate of Deluge geology. As a member of the Sacred History Research Expedition, he had eagerly and enthusiastically reached out for any and all information, no matter how trivial, that might tend to prove this explanation of geological phenomena. Collecting information that would possibly lead to a rediscovery of Noah's ark was part of it; at least, that is, in the beginning.

It soon developed into a mania.

Hiding securely behind the paintless walls of his trailer, parked in a backyard on Grand Avenue in Los Angeles, Allen's often dictatorial manner and erratic behavior eventually caused some of his cosearchers and acquaintances to look for ways to discredit his methods. It is hard to prove whether this sparked the unfavorable publicity surrounding the first officially published "eyewitness account." The few facts Allen leaked to Floyd Gurley, editor of the *New Eden Magazine*, a tract published in Los Angeles, gave Gurley sufficient ground to print a story entitled "Noah's Ark Found," crediting it to a Russian named Vladimir Roskovitsky.

Within days the story made the rounds of the religious press and was hailed as the first modern evidence that Noah's ark was indeed still on Mount Ararat.

The following is the story in its original shape:

NOAH'S ARK FOUND

by Vladimir Roskovitsky

"It was in the days just before the Russian Revolution that this story really began.

"A group of us Russian aviators were stationed at a lonely temporary air outpost about twenty-five miles northeast of Mount Ararat.

"The day was dry and terribly hot as August days so often are in this semi-desert land. Even the lizards were flattened out under the shady sides of rocks or twigs, their mouths open and tongues occasionally lashing out as if each panting breath would be their last. Only occasionally would a tiny wisp of air rattle the parched vegetation and stir up a choking cloudlet of dust.

"Far up the side of the mountain we could see a thundershower, while still further up we could see the white snow cap of Mount Ararat, which has snow all the year around because of its great height. How we longed for some of that snow!

"Then the miracle happened. The captain walked in and announced that plane number seven had its supercharger installed and was ready for high altitude tests and ordered my buddy and I to make the tests. At last we could escape the heat!

"Needless to say, we wasted no time getting on our parachutes, strapping on our oxygen cans, and doing all the half dozen other little things that have to be done before 'going up.'

"Then a climb into the cockpits, safety belts fastened, a mechanic gives the prop a flip and yells, 'Contact,' and in less time than it takes to tell it we were in the air. No use wasting time warming up the engine when the sun already had it nearly red hot.

"We circled the field several times until we hit the fourteen-thousand-foot-mark and then stopped climbing for a few minutes to get used to the altitude.

"I looked over to the right at that beautiful snow-capped peak, now just a little above us, and for some reason I can't explain, turned and headed the plane straight toward it.

"My buddy turned around and looked at me with question marks in his eyes, but there was too much noise for him to ask questions. After all, twenty-five miles doesn't mean much at a hundred miles an hour.

"As I looked down at the great stone battlements surrounding the lower part of the mountain, I remembered having heard that it had never been climbed since the year seven hundred before Christ, when some pilgrims were supposed to have gone up there to scrape tar off of an old shipwreck to make good luck emblems to wear around their necks to prevent their crops being destroyed by excessive rainfall. The legend said they had left in haste after a bolt of lightning struck near them, and had never returned. Silly ancients! Who ever heard of looking for a shipwreck on a mountaintop?

"A couple of circles around the snow-capped dome and then a long swift glide down the south side and then we suddenly came upon a perfect little gem of a lake; blue as an emerald, but still frozen over on the shady side. We circled round and returned for another look at it.

"Suddenly my companion whirled around and yelled something, and excitedly pointed down at the overflow end of the lake. I looked and nearly fainted!

"A submarine? No, it wasn't, for it had stubby masts, but the top was rounded over with only a flat catwalk about five feet across down the length of it. What a strange craft, built as though the designer had expected the waves to roll over the top most of the time and had engineered it to wallow in the sea like a log, with those stubby masts carrying only enough sail to keep it facing the waters.

"We flew down as close as safety permitted and took several circles around it. We were surprised when we got close to it at the immense size of the thing, for it was as long as a city block and would compare very favorably in size to the modern battleships of today. It was grounded on the shore of the lake with about one fourth of the rear end still running out into the water, and its extreme rear was three fourths under water. It had been partly dismantled on one side near the front, and on the other side there was a great door nearly twenty feet square, but with the door gone. This seemed quite out of proportion, as even today ships seldom have doors even half that large.

"After seeing all we could see from the air, we broke all speed records back down to the airport.

"When we related our find, the laughter was loud and long. Some accused us of getting drunk on too much oxygen, and there were many other remarks too numerous to relate.

"The captain, however, was serious. He asked several questions and ended by saying, 'Take me up there, I want to look at it.'

"We made the trip without incident and returned to the airport.

" 'What do you make of it?' I asked, as we climbed out of the plane.

" 'Astounding,' he replied. 'Do you know what ship that is?'

" 'Of course not, sir.'

" 'Ever heard of Noah's ark?'

" 'Yes, sir, but I don't understand what the legend of Noah's ark has to do with us finding this strange thing fourteen thousand feet up on a mountain top.'

"'This strange craft,' explained the captain, 'is Noah's ark. It has been sitting up there for nearly five thousand years. Being frozen up for nine or ten months of the year, it couldn't rot and has been in cold storage, as it were, all this time. You have made the most amazing discovery of the age.'

"When the captain sent his report to the Russian government, it aroused considerable interest, and the Czar sent two special companies of soldiers to climb the mountain. One group of fifty men attacked one side and the other group of one hundred men attacked the mountain from the other side.

"Two weeks of hard work were required to chop out a trail along the cliffs of the lower part of the mountain, and it was nearly a month before the ark was reached.

"Complete measurements were taken and plans drawn of it as well as many photographs, all of which were sent to the Czar of Russia.

"The ark was found to contain hundreds of small rooms and some rooms very large with high ceilings. The large rooms usually had a fence of great timbers across them, some of which were two feet thick, as though designed to hold beasts ten times as large as elephants. Other rooms were lined with tiers of cages somewhat like one sees today at a poultry show, only instead of chicken wire, they had rows of tiny wrought iron bars along the fronts.

"Everything was heavily painted with a waxlike paint resembling shellac, and the workmanship of the craft showed all the signs of a high type of civilization.

"The wood used throughout was oleander, which belongs to the cypress family and never rots, which, of course, coupled with the facts of it being painted and it being frozen most of the time, accounted for its perfect preservation.

"The expedition found on the peak of the mountain above

the ship, the burned remains of the timbers which were missing out of the one side of the ship. It seems that these timbers had been hauled up to the top of the peak and used to build a tiny one-room shrine, inside of which was a rough stone hearth like the altars the Hebrews use for sacrifices, and it had either caught fire from the altar or had been struck by lightning, as the timbers were considerably burned and charred over and the roof was completely burned off.

"A few days after this expedition sent its report to the Czar, the government was overthrown and godless Bolshevism took over, so that the records were never made public and probably were destroyed in the zeal of the Bolsheviks to discredit all religion and belief in the truth of the Bible.

"We, White Russians of the air fleet, escaped through Armenia, and four of us came to America, where we could be free to live according to the 'good Old Book,' which we had seen for ourselves to be absolutely true, even to as fantastic sounding a thing as a world flood."*

The resulting inquiries that poured into the office of the *New Eden Magazine* were all referred to Benjamin Allen, who soon wished he had never heard of Floyd Gurley or the magazine. What Allen had confided to Gurley in confidence had now become public knowledge—and now for the first time Allen began a serious investigation of the leads and bits of information on which he had built his basic story. It is not known exactly when and from whom Benjamin Allen received his first facts regarding the Russian expedition; but from correspondence found in his file, it became evident that it was the Roskovitsky account in the *New Eden Magazine* that forced him into action. In a conversation I had with him in the immediate postwar years, he recalled that he had first heard of the basic Russian story a few years prior to the outbreak of World War II. From memory, based on his con-

*Taken from *New Eden Magazine* and various other pamphlets.

versations with people who claimed to be relatives of two of the soldiers of the expedition, he pieced the story together and "loaned" it to Floyd Gurley. But the account in *New Eden* set his temper flaring. Drawing upon his prewar contacts, he set upon enlarging his initial leads; this time, however, by mail, and a number of answers were received confirming what he had heard years before.

Wrote James Frazer on April 4, 1940:

"Your letter, dated March 30, is at hand, in regard to the ark of Noah. Yes, my father-in-law, John Schilleroff, told me at different times about the ark of Noah, but he did not mention any landmarks, though he did mention the town he started from. I could not pronounce the name and have forgotten it. He was German and I do not speak German. He died some years ago.

"Mr. John Jorgensen, a Dane, formerly my neighbor here, now also deceased, told me the same story, he also having served in the Russian army in the Ararat region. They had never met, though their accounts fully agree. They belonged to different expeditions and went at different times. They were both sober and reliable men, and therefore I believe their story. The following is the story as they both told it to me:

"While in the Russian army, they were ordered to pack for a long tramp up into the mountains of Ararat. A Russian aviator had sighted what looked to him like a huge wooden structure in a small lake.

"About two thirds of the way up, probably a little farther, they stopped on a high cliff, and in a small valley below them was a dense swamp in which this object could be seen. It appeared as a huge ship or barge with one end under water, and only one corner could be clearly seen from where these men stood. Some went closer, and especially the captain. They could not get out to it because of the water and the many poisonous snakes and insects. The captain told them all the details.

"I'll do all I can to find others who were in those exploring parties and let you know."

Nothing has ever been received indicating that this was done —except for one letter which arrived in support of Frazer's account. This again was another piece of hearsay material with nothing to support or substantiate its basic supposition. Sadly, this marked the end of the trail for Benjamin Allen's feeble attempt to uncover facts that would corroborate his story, but for inexplainable reasons, he waited until October 17, 1945, to disassociate himself from the *New Eden* account. His defense was contained in an open letter mailed from his trailer at 219 North Grand Avenue, Los Angeles:

"One of the most exaggerated accounts of the Ark was published in 1940 by Mr. Gurley in one of his booklets called the 'New Eden' which he printed in that year," Allen stated, finally recognizing that his reputation was at stake. "In conversation with him I had given him the few details originating from two soldiers in the Czarist Russian army during the First World War, deceased many years ago. The story by these soldiers came to me from their relatives of how a Russian aviator had sighted a suspicious looking structure in one of Ararat's obscure canyons. Infantrymen were sent on foot to investigate and their officers, and they decided it must be Noah's ark, with one end sunk in a small swamp. *These were the only details they gave.* Being a geologist worker, I had investigated and speculated on how the ark could have been saved by glaciation till recent times in view of the sudden origin and subsequent history of glaciation. To Mr. Gurley I gave some of these ideas, very briefly. I had no idea he was publishing anything. I told him plainly that the story from the soldiers was by no means worthy of publication till it could be corroborated from other sources. But, *without my knowledge and consent,* he concocted a masterpiece of fiction and invention and published it as though it were true in every detail. About 95% is pure fiction, but the meager details from the former soldiers could be true. The name Roskovitsky and the *person* are pure fiction, *as are all parts but the few I have given here.* With the geological ideas I gave him, he could construct a very plausible story, which has 'deluged' the credulous world.

"I soon began to be deluged with letters asking about the reliability of this wild story, (as it was generally known that I had been conducting research and publishing articles on the folklore and archaeology of the Deluge), and letters are still coming. The story has been constantly published by the radical religious press, and even by some of the secular papers, with a constant addition of 'embellishments.' However, much harm began to be done to me, and has increased, because word got out that what real data there was in it came from me, and I am being charged by some with the whole fabrication. Much harm has been done also to the religious press, and the cause of the Bible truth. At my request it has been widely repudiated by many religious papers.

"Soon after his story appeared, a woman here in Los Angeles told one that 'lays it in the shade' for skill and inventive genius. After a year of careful checking we found that this one was 'out of the whole cloth.' This story is a 'gem' of its kind, but was never published so far as I know. Beware of still other accounts that are floating around *without any key by which they can be checked.*

"The following is a letter from Mr. Gurley which he wrote at my request on October 17, 1945, but which he wished to date back to 1940 when the incidents occurred:

" 'Los Angeles, Calif.,
" 'August 1, 1940

" 'To Whom It May Concern:"

" 'This is to certify that I, Floyd Millard Gurley, did publish in the *New Eden Magazine* (of which I am the editor) an article about the finding of Noah's Ark on Mt. Ararat.

" 'All of the basic material used in that article came from the researches of Mr. Benjamin Franklin Allen, and the article was written up in story form with the intent of making it more interesting to read.

" 'Apologies are hereby offered to Mr. Allen for having used some of his material which he feels was not sufficiently corroborated and which he states he does not wish to release for publication at this date.

[signed]

" 'Floyd M. Gurley' "

But that wasn't the end of Gurley's apologies.

In a letter dated November 10, 1945, he repeated his apology in answer to an inquiry by Dr. A. J. Smith, the man who in later years became president of the Oriental Archaeological Research Expedition.

"Yes," he confessed in that letter, "I am the originator of the story which I wrote up to the best of my ability from secondhand facts.

"I published it, for the first time, in the New Eden Magazine of which I am the editor."

On October 6, 1945, this episode received new life when the White Russian publication *Rosseya* published a story dealing with the reported discovery of Noah's ark. It contained all the overtones of the original Russian aviator-sighting story, but what made it more interesting were the minute details concerning the number of soldiers who participated in the follow-up expeditions and the resulting activities. There was a striking similarity to the *New Eden* story, for the aviator who had discovered the strange craft in the *Rosseya* account also thought it to be a submarine. It, too, was leaning on its side toward the shore of a small lake, and its door was also missing. Not until the following year did the Czar, according to the story, dispatch an expedition to the mountain to lay claim to the ark. The article revealed that two research divisions of 150 infantrymen, army engineers, and other specialists finally approached the object after a full month of difficult ascent, fighting the hazards of falling rocks and sudden blizzards. The article related how, when the party reached the ark, "without a word of command everyone took off his hat, looking reverently toward the ark; everybody knew, feeling it in his heart and soul," that they were standing before the actual ark of Noah.

With painstaking accuracy, measurements were taken by the team of engineers. They found that the ship was about 500 feet long, having a width of about 83 feet in the widest place. The height, too, proved to follow the Bible proportions, for it was the anticipated 50 feet. The inside also confirmed what had been expected. The ship throughout had been divided into cages and rooms to house the various animals during the sojourn on the angry waves. As to the reasons for its surviving more than 4,000 years since the Flood, the story emphasized that "the ark was covered from inside as well as from outside with some kind of dark brown color, which was identified as 'wax and varnish.'" An on-the-site analysis of the 4,000-year-old wood proved it to be of the cypress family, and, to complete the story, the party also found the altar erected by Noah after he left the ark.

What happened to the maps, photographs, wood samples, and the report?

The story had a fitting answer. It was taken by a special courier to the chief of staff of the White Russian Army, but before he was able to reach the general, he was intercepted by the Bolsheviks and shot. Trotsky, himself, the tale goes, was the final recipient of the material, and he had it destroyed.

It would have been excellent evidence. However, with no proof, it became only a story, not much more.

But wait—how about the writer? It was left to Eryl Cummings, president of the Sacred History Research Expedition, to track him down. Following a lead furnished him by *Rosseya,* he flew to Seattle for a meeting with a former White Russian General, Alexander Jacob Elshin, the man who the editors of *Rosseya* claimed was the author of the ark-discovery narrative.

But put under kind pressure, he soon passed the responsibility.

"I didn't write it," he said to Eryl in a soft, smiling way. "My friend Koor, Colonel Alexander Koor—he wrote it. I'll give you an introduction to see him." A meeting with Koor followed, and judging from documents he supplied, he pulled out all stops and furnished information that he had somehow neglected to include in the *Rosseya* account.

On March 1, 1946, he submitted the following data:

"Here are some data which should help our research, from the official records of the Russian Caucasian Army, 1914-1917, by General E. B. Maslovsky.

"The headquarters of the 14th Railroad Battalion was at Bayazit, just southwest of Greater Ararat, with Brigade Headquarters at Maku, southeast of Lesser Ararat, commanded by Col. Sverczkoff. The 14th Battalion came to the front in the summer of 1916, from Russia. I understand that the discovery of Noah's Ark was in the end of 1916, with the scouting parties having to wait until the summer of 1917.

"I know that Sergeant Boris V. Rujansky belonged to the 14th Battalion. I understand, and it is logical, that the first and second parties of the expedition to Mount Ararat were formed from the local force of the 14th Battalion of #D Zomorsky Brigade, by order from the local Brigade Headquarters. Sergeant B. V. Rujansky was sent to join the party because he was a specialist. Before the war he worked in the Technological Institute of Peter the Great, and attended the Imperial Institute of Archaeology in Saint Petersburg. In 1916 the 3-D Caucasian Aviation Detachment, under the command of 1st Lt. Zobolotsky, served air duty over the region of Mount Ararat, Lake Van, and Lake Urmia. This aviation detachment served the 4th Caucasian Corps, and the Army Aviation Inspector was Captain Koorbatoff. I hope 1st Lt. Zabolotsky is the man you are looking for, for he, from an airplane, sighted the ark and started the investigation. Captain Koorbatoff was his supervisor. . . .

"I was in the Ararat region in November, 1915, during the war between Turkey and Russia. The general headquarters of the Caucasian Army sent me and other officers in command of emergency forces from Barzem and Pytergorsky for protection of the Araratsky Pass, just northwest of the peak of Greater Ararat and Zorsky Pass a few miles northwest, from the imminent Turkish attack.

"In June and July the 3rd Turkish Army had broken through our forces very close to . . . Mount Ararat.

"It was during this military service that I learned of the several undeciphered inscriptions and investigated archaeological sites in that region."

Of more interest, however, was the statement Colonel Koor provided concerning the 1916 Russian expedition—the one that caused all the excitement.

"To Whom It May Concern: This is to certify that I, Alexander A. Koor, former colonel and chief-in-command, of the 19th Petropaulovsky Regiment, heard the following concerning the discovery of Noah's Ark:

"(1) 1st Lt. Paul Vasilivich Rujansky of the 156th Elisavetpolsky Regiment, Caucasian Army. I knew all of Rujansky's family for years. I met them in the city of Kazan, Russia, where I attended the government military academy. 1st Lt. Rujansky was wounded in Erzerum when his regiment took Chaban Dede, central fort of the Erzerum fortifications. He was relieved from active duty and sent to work in the commandant's office, in the city of Irkustsk, Siberia. After the Bolsheviks made an uprising he moved to the city of Harbin, Manchuria, where I found him in 1921.

"(2) Lt. Peter Nicolovich Leslin of the 261st Ahilchinsky Regiment, also of the Caucasian Army. During the Bolshevik uprising he was arrested but escaped from them, and in December, 1918, he joined my Petropaulovsky Regiment.

"(3) About July or August, 1921, I and Lt. Leslin met 1st Lt.

Rujansky in Harbin. During our conversations, 1st Lt. Rujansky told me about the discovery of Noah's Ark. He (1st Lt. Rujansky) didn't know about the details because he was wounded and sent to Russia, but he knew because his brother, Boris Vasilivich Rujansky, Sergeant of the Military Railroad Battalion, was a member of the investigating party which was sent to Mount Ararat to corroborate the discovery of Noah's Ark.

"Lt. Leslin admitted he had also heard about the discovery of Noah's Ark, not as a rumor but as news, from the senior adjutant of his division, who had told him that Noah's Ark was found in the saddle of two peaks of Mount Ararat.

"This is all I heard from these two officers, and I am sure both told me the truth.

"(Signed) Col. Alexander A. Koor."

As nice as it would be to have complete confidence in this account, there are several disturbing factors that continually arise. Those who have known Colonel Koor intimately during his exile in the United States vouch for his integrity, but the questions remain. Why, for example, did Colonel Koor wait until 1945 before submitting his knowledge about the whereabouts of the ark to public scrutiny? Political exiles as a rule are not in the millionaire bracket, and Colonel Koor was no exception. Arriving in the United States in the early 20's as a Russian escapee, he was undoubtedly in need of both friends and money; yet he practically sat on the greatest story of all time, completely ignoring its value in a Christian land. Assuredly he could have gained stature and importance by using the ark story, for judging from the *Rosseya* account, his knowledge of the Russian discovery must have been quite detailed—almost *too* detailed for someone who had only heard about it from casual acquaintances. Is it possible that he was not aware of this account before he became exposed to the *New Eden* story? It seems probable that he could have "borrowed" the *New Eden* account and enlarged on it, spiking it with details that could only be added by someone familiar with the territory and the identification of the troops in the area at that time.

Having served in the Ararat region during the first world war, and with an avid interest in archaeology, he was a man who already possessed the basic ingredients for a great story. The *New Eden* feature could have served as his outline for the *Rosseya* article, thereby enabling him to recapture some of the glory that was his during the time of the Czar. It does not seem likely that this discovery story could have remained hidden that long by a man who had everything to gain from revealing the whereabouts of the world's oldest ship.

As much as Colonel Koor's *Rosseya* article rests on hearsay and possible fantasy, so my judgment rests on a suspicion of plagiarism and faith in the unfailing sequence found in the law of cause and result—*New Eden* being the cause, *Rosseya* the result.

Nearly all pamphlets ever written on the reported discovery of Noah's ark mention Prince Nouri, archdeacon of Babylon and apostolic leader of Nestorian Christians, as one of the original finders of the ark.

Who was Nouri?

As in the case with most stories written about him by those lacking the necessary information, either his name is misspelled or his ecclesiastical title is magnified or altered, or additional titles have been added to the already impressive list. There is certainly sufficient grounds for all of these mistakes, as he was indeed a rather mysterious personality.

Nouri first appeared in Western headlines when, during the Chicago World's Fair in 1893, he attempted to raise enough funds to have the ark—which he claimed to have discovered—disassembled and transported to the Fair for exhibit.

With flair and theatrics, Nouri startled the gathered industrialists and theologians by asking them to finance an expedition to haul the ark down the mountainside and reconstruct it again like a gigantic jigsaw puzzle during the Fair. Cynicism prevailed over commercialism, and Nouri vanished, shaken by so much unbelief. The shimmering heat of skepticism had forced him to retreat into his world of supposed ecclesiastical greatness.

Where he actually came from no one really knew, and it took detailed research even to uncover the barest facts concerning him. His critics still insist that Nouri never really existed, and that the man who claimed to be Prince Nouri was just an impoverished actor masquerading as a holy man. Others called him a complete fake; a hoax that was to be perpetrated on the assembled money-bags for the sake of a gigantic swindle.

But Archdeacon Nouri did exist, and so does his assertion of having discovered the ark of Noah.

The late Frederick B. Coan, D.D., a missionary who worked for more than forty years in the Near East, left some pertinent facts relating to the mystery man. In his book *Yesterdays in Persia and Kurdistan,* recalling his experiences, Coan writes: "One is apt to meet with some very interesting characters in the East, one of whom comes to mind and is worth describing.

"About 35 years ago . . . one of our Assyrian friends told us of a very interesting guest who had dropped in on him by the name of Archbishop Nouri. He had come from Malabar in southern India, where there are today (1939) some 500,000 Nestorians, a remnant of the work of the Nestorian missionaries, who in the very early centuries carried the Gospel to India and far beyond. Archdeacon Nouri said he had been sent by them to be consecrated Bishop over them by the Nestorian Patriarch Mar-Shimun, who, as Patriarch of all the Nestorians in Kurdistan and Persia, lived at Kochanis, Turkey, five days travel from Urmia. . . .

"Now for the story of his wonderful discovery of the Ark. He said he had made three attempts to scale Mount Ararat before he succeeded. At last his toil was rewarded and he stood overwhelmed as he saw the old Ark there wedged between two rocks and half filled with snow and ice. He got inside, where measurements coincided exactly with the account given in the sixth chapter of Genesis.

"We invited him to give a lecture on his marvelous discovery in the College chapel, and missionaries, teachers, and students filled the place and were most deeply interested. He sincerely believed he had seen the Ark and almost convinced others he had.

"He had gone to Belgium and tried to organize a company to take it to Chicago to the World's Fair, but they felt the risks of such a long journey were too great, in addition to the heavy cost of transporting it so far. He was much disappointed, for he knew it would be a great attraction, and that people from all over the world would go to see it. So there it lies."

Nouri's consecration as bishop, mentioned by Coan in his book, never took place. His request went unheeded when he knocked on the door of the patriarchal palace.

The Rev. Sadook de MarShimun, after having heard from his uncle Deacon Shlimun de MarShimun, commented regarding Nouri in a communication in late November, 1945: "He came there to visit His Beatitude Ruel Shimun XIX, the Patriarch of the East, for his episcopal ordination and his recognition as the bishop of the Syrian Nestorian Church of Malabar, South India; and that Nouri went to Urmia, Persia, after his request was rejected by the Patriarch."

So it seems that Nouri did exist. At least Dr. J. O. Kinneman, Director of the Bureau of Bible Research in Long Beach, California, thought so. He wrote: "At the World's Parliament of Religions, World's Fair, Chicago, Illinois, in 1893, I had the honor, the pleasure of meeting Dr. Nouri personally, and conversing with him several times. There is no mistake that he actually lived, walked, and talked upon earth, for I am sure I was not talking to a ghost."*

---

*Communication on file.

Those who have examined the various reports dealing with Nouri will readily admit that the man did live, but to me it is not his *existence* that is at stake; it is his claim to have found Noah's ark. Opponents of the Nouri account have ample reasons to doubt his reliability. A letter written August 11, 1945, by Mrs. Elizabeth E. Verbrycke explains why:

"At the time of the Chicago exhibition in 1893," she reports, "Dr. Nouri was invited to the Parliament of Religions held in the summer of 1893 in Chicago under the leadership of Dr. J. Barrows, pastor of the First Presbyterian Church of that city.

"Dr. Nouri accepted and spoke to the congress of religions and delivered many lectures on Noah's ark, his discoveries of the Mountains of the Moon, etc. He then proceeded westward, reaching San Francisco. While there, my father and mother met him and were impressed by his looks, manner, and deep consecration. My father came east as a delegate to a meeting of the General Assembly held in Washington, D.C.

"While he was in the east, my mother received a letter from him (Nouri) written from the Napa Insane Asylum of California, asking if she could not get him liberated.

"It seems that while in San Francisco he fell into the hands of thieves who robbed him of all his beautiful jewels, robes, in fact everything he had. To cover up their crime, they cast him into the asylum. He was not insane, but it was almost enough to make him so, all alone in a foreign land. My mother went to Napa, California Insane Asylum and said she would be responsible for him.

"So as he was destitute he lived in my father's home for weeks, maybe months, as it was the day before registered mail, post office money orders, and telegraph facilities for quick communication, all mail having to go by slow steamers both ways."

Quite a life for a young archdeacon, for at the time of his asylum experience he was only twenty-eight years old, having been born in Baghdad on February 7, 1865, as the Earl of the

Great House of Nouri. Even his titles could not save him—yet they were undoubtedly impressive. While today they would have created mildly suppressed chuckles, in his day, he proudly displayed his titles wherever he went.

Sacred Crown's Supreme Representative-General of the Holy Orthodox Patriarchal Imperiality; His Pontifical Eminence, the Most Venerable Prelate Monseignor, the Zamorrin Nouri, John Joseph, Prince of Nouri, DD, LLD (by Divine Providence), Chaldean Patriarchal Archdeacon of Babylon and Jerusalem, Grand Apostolic Ambassador of Malabar, India, and Persia. The discoverer of Noah's Ark and the Golden Mountains of the Moon —these are only part of the titles he claimed. Others more flowery were no doubt kept in reserve in case the usual ones failed to generate the necessary impression.

The use of these titles suggest that Christian humility was not the outstanding trait of the Prince of Nouri. Even if his claim to have located Noah's ark was true, this display of conceit and pride from the twenty-eight-year-old archdeacon most assuredly alienated the assembled clergymen in Chicago. His personality puzzled not only strangers but also his friends. One lady, while working as a Presbyterian missionary in Urmia, Persia (presently known as Rezia), met him at the home of friends and later commented on his visit in her diary dated, March 9, 1896:

"Archdeacon Nouri was sent for," she confided to the book.

"He is a Chaldean from Baghdad, who is now on a mission from the Malabar Christians to MarShimun [for his coronation?], and claims to have discovered Noah's Ark, also to have found gold in the Mountains of the Moon, to have been in almost all of the countries of the world, and to know fourteen languages. He speaks English very well and is most entertaining.

"The greatest part of him is his supernatural conceit. He claims to have been put wrongfully in an insane asylum in California, but it is very easy to believe that he may have been insane. His descriptions of his feelings at that time are very vivid."

Later that year Archbishop Nouri, who had announced in March that he was on his way to Kochanis, Turkey, for his coronation, was seen in Cairo, Egypt, where he renewed his acquaintance with Dr. and Mrs. Barrows, having previously met them at the Chicago World's Fair in 1893. Mrs. Barrows wrote about this second meeting in her diary dated September 25, 1896 and mentioned that Prince Nouri told them again about his discovery of Noah's ark and of his scheduled coronation as Patriarch of the Chaldean Church. The question is, why, if he was traveling from Urmia, Persia, to Kochanis, Turkey, in March of that year, did he land in Cairo in September of the same year, *still* on the way to Kochanis? It is not the time element that is puzzling, but the geography. To travel from Urmia to Kochanis via Cairo is like going from New York to Kansas City by way of Miami or journeying from Amsterdam to Vienna by way of Madrid. This means that Nouri's sojourn in Cairo was not exactly a stop on the way to his coronation. And what about the quotation from Dr. Coan's book a few pages back in which Coan mentioned that Nouri was en route to be crowned bishop by the Nestorian Patriarch MarShimun? The book was written in 1939 and the meeting in which *this* was told occurred 35 years prior to 1939, thereby placing Nouri's claim to his imminent coronation to the year 1904—coronation which was "forthcoming" as far back as 1893.

Nouri existed; there is no doubt about that. But was he sane? Were his claims reliable? It is difficult to believe that the thieves who robbed him then had him committed to an insane asylum. Why didn't they just forget about him once they had taken what they were after? Why bother to lock him up? Also, why would Nouri still maintain his obvious obsession of "imminent coronation" as late as 1904, while it had eluded him since 1893? It is inconceivable that for such an important occasion as coronation to bishop, he deemed it necessary to travel from Persia to Turkey via Europe and the United States, all the while forcing the Nestorian Patriarch MarShimun to wait and wait.

Is it possible that when his request for the coronation was rejected, he could and would not accept this new reality and retreated in a dream world which eventually landed him in the Napa insane asylum?

It is also strange that, aside from his claim that he had located and seen the ark, he did not divulge any pertinent details surrounding the discovery. Does that seem to be the story of a man who had actually viewed Noah's ark?

I, for one, am willing to run ahead of the relentless judgment of the future historians and cast serious doubts on the reliability of Nouri as a discoverer of the ark.

Even though Ararat is regarded as a holy mountain by the Armenians and many flood traditions have originated in this mountainous region, the actual eye-witness accounts that have reached the Western world from Armenia are relatively few.

There may be many reasons for this. Perhaps the native Kurds have accepted the presence of the shiplike object as a natural phenomenon—something that belongs to the mountain. Possibly because of this they simply don't care. Or could it be that the remoteness of the object has limited its exposure to merely a few of the mountain people? Another reason may be that no one likes to be ridiculed, least of all unlettered locals, and because of that some stories are better remembered than told.

Whatever the reason, there is little doubt that many eyewitness accounts have drowned in the centuries of time while others have simply been suppressed.

The story of Haji Yearam is one of the few Armenian sightings that managed to reach the West, giving the outside world a glimpse of what the ark must have looked like to a young Armenian boy.

It was a Protestant minister, Pastor H. N. Williams, who first brought Haji's story to the ark searchers. Shortly before his death in May, 1920, Haji Yearam told his story, committing his recollection to the annals of ark history.

Weak from dysentery and near death, Haji laboriously breathed the words that unveiled his memory, revealing the adventures of a young man who, after a pilgrimage from Ararat to Jerusalem, became known to his friends as Haji Yearam, Jeremiah the Pilgrim.

Whispering softly, he told of his early years where tradition had taught him about the angels who, as the Flood subsided, guided the ark into a haven of rest among the peaks of Greater Ararat.

Drawing on his conversation with Haji, Pastor Williams recalled how he told him of the early pilgrimages that had been conducted to the ark for centuries after the Flood and how Armenian tradition indicates that the followers of Noah carved steps into the mountainside, and yearly throngs of followers would climb the steep mountain steps and gather about the ark for worship services.

"It was a gradual cold that followed the Flood which finally froze the ark into a lake on the great mountain," Haji Yearam's story goes, "but it was the effect of a devastating storm which finally buried the ark completely. The lightning and torrential rains which accompanied the storm also obliterated the trail up the mountain."

According to Haji, this marked the end of the annual pilgrimages, because it created the superstition that God did not want the ark disturbed.

"Yet they handed down by tradition the supposed near location of the ark," Mr. Williams's account continued. "The few who saw it from time to time in very hot summers declared that its prow still extended out at the end of the glacier into the stream that melted and ran down the mountain. Very few people were hardy enough to scale the mountain, but from time to time shepherds in hot summers approached the site and in fear told a few others what they had seen.

"When young Yearam was a large boy, nearly grown, three

strange men and their hired helpers came to their humble mountain home. They were atheists. They had organized an expedition at great sacrifice and expense for the specific purpose of exploring Greater Ararat to prove that there was no evidence that Noah's ark ever rested there. They at last persuaded the father of young Yearam to be their official guide, since he had always lived at the base and on the side of the great mountain and knew the country very intimately.

"Young Yearam had not yet made his pilgrimage to Jerusalem to become a haji. Since he was strong and curious and willing, he was hired as an assistant to his father who was to be their guide.

"The summer was unusually hot," the story continues. "The expedition reorganized and located camps and posted supply stations, etc. At last the final ascent was under way, and the last part of it was scaled by the three atheists, guided and helped by young Yearam and his father.

"At last, up there thousands of feet, but below the summit and in a sort of bowl or valley, surrounded by a group of peaks, they came to the glacier that once had been a mountain lake.

"There at the end of the lake where the stream poured down the mountain from the glacier, the ice had melted and there the prow of a mighty ship protruded out of the ice. In the side of the great ship there was a doorway, but the door was missing. The ship was covered outside with a thick layer of pitch or varnish. They entered the ship by the door and inside the ship was covered with that layer of lacquer or pitch the same as it was on the outside.

"There were cages of all sizes inside, many of them having great strong bars like great animal cages. They could not see far inside because they did not have lanterns or torches. But they saw enough to know it was none other than the mighty ship called Noah's ark.

"The atheists were at first amazed and dumbfounded. Then

they grew bitter and angry and violent. They told their guide and his son that they would keep tabs on them. To save their lives they promised never to tell.

"The guide and his son kept their lips closed through the years for fear of their lives. The atheists reported to all whom they met that there were no evidences of any ship on the mountain, or any remains of any such thing and that the tradition was only vain imagination.

"These men were much older than the young assistant guide. He had become a "haji," had been a merchant in Constantinople, and had traveled in Europe and America. It had now been over half a century and he had never heard anything from these men. Haji was now an old man, and he felt sure that these wicked men must be dead or too old to do him any harm."

Williams then continued by telling how Haji had asked him to write the story down and read it back to him so as to avoid any mistakes in the account.

Even though Haji Yearam died soon thereafter, Pastor Williams lived on; in fact, even today, in 1974, he maintains good health and still adheres to the story as told him by the old haji. What happened to the written account? As with most of the evidence that could substantiate many old eyewitness accounts, it disappeared. But Mr. Williams adds more to the story.

"Three years after Haji Yearam had me write carefully his story, and after he was dead and buried," Williams relates, "I sat in my home in Brockton reading a newspaper. There was printed a deathbed confession of a noted scientist of former years. He died in London, England. Before he died he said he had to make a confession because he did not dare die until he told the truth.

"He said his two companions were dead, so he was responsible to no one but God. He confessed that he was convinced that there is a God and that the Bible is His Word.

"He then told the story of the expedition he and two other

atheists had made to Ararat and that they had discovered Noah's ark.

"This man, before he died, told the same story, gave the same dates as Haji Yearam had given me to record in California when he knew he was soon to die.

"I pasted the newspaper account in the composition book," he went on, "together with the record I had made for Haji Yearam."

But in 1940 a tragedy occurred when a sudden explosion and the resulting fire destroyed Williams's house.

"Everything we had in the world, but our lives, was burned to ashes, except our bodies, and they were terribly burned and injured," he recalled.

What about the Haji Yearam story?

That too burned—destroying the only official account of the deathbed confession of an old man.

Eryl Cummings, dean of the "ark-eologists," pursued this story vigorously. Soon after Cummings became acquainted with it, Williams added more details in letters to Cummings. It was the death certificate of Haji, however, that provided the first clue that would help to date the expedition. Issued by the Bureau of Vital Statistics, it indicated that at death Haji had been 82 years old, establishing his year of birth as 1838. His date of death had been registered as May 3, 1920. This confirmed the fact that he would have been a "large boy not yet fully grown" around 1850-1856. Stubborn attempts to trace the deathbed confession story proved fruitless, but several expeditions to Mount Ararat have been traced to that time period, even though their exact composition and membership is rather obscure. Fernand Navarra once mentioned having received a call from "a Frenchman whose grandfather had participated in an expedition to Ararat under Napoleon III, and had brought back a piece of wood given to him as a gift from the natives." Judging from history, this must have taken place sometime during 1852-1870. Danby Seymour, an Englishman, is also reported to have ascended the mountain with a small group of fellow Britishers in 1856, while other reports reveal Major Stuart as leader of another expedition. However, all efforts to locate the "deathbed confession" was of no avail. Many people were found who claimed to have read the story, but no one in fact remembered the actual newspaper. In the one case where a reader did recall the name of the paper, the right copy could not be located. No confirmation of the Haji Yearam account has ever been uncovered. It still remains hearsay. With the exception of the one minister and two relatives who are willing to authenticate his version of the written story destroyed in the fire, no trace of it can be found.

Both the nineteenth and twentieth centuries have been fertile years for ark stories. As a nation lying on the doorstep of the inscrutable East, Turkey has retained many facets of its unfathomable and mysterious past. One of these is its inflexible insistence on keeping official records classified and hidden under a permanent cloak of secrecy, even though the records are often outdated and of no strategic value whatsoever.

This policy has proved to be a major obstacle in tracing any event relating to a possible discovery of the ark.

While scientific institutions outside of Turkey reported a minor earth tremor and subsequent landslides in the Ararat mountains during 1883, Turkey maintained official silence, treating the widely recorded disturbance as a state secret. The only facts concerning the earthquake that are available to researchers are those given in the newspaper reports of that year.

The reason the official files are of vital importance is that all of the published stories mention that a team of Turkish commissioners, sent to the mountain to investigate the possible damage caused by the resulting landslides, stumbled upon an object resembling a huge ship and "identified" it as Noah's ark.

The *Nieuwe Rotterdamsche Courant,* an influential newspaper in The Netherlands, was the first to break the news to the West. In a dispatch dated July 28, 1883, it reported:

"From Armenia comes the news of a strange find. In a glacier on the Mount of Ararat, nothing less has been discovered than the Ark of Noah, not in a seaworthy, but nevertheless well preserved, state.

"The wood is gopher wood, according to the Bible story. It is reported that an American has already started negotiations with the local Pasha for the purchase of the relic."

In the United States two major papers, Chicago *Tribune* and the New York *Herald* commented on the discovery the same day, August 10, 1883, although completely different in style and intent. The *Herald* account appeared under the title "Ararat's Antique":

"Now let the heathen rage and the free thinkers call on their respective beer cellars to hide them, for has not Noah's Ark been discovered, and right on the mountain where she discharged her cargo and passengers more than 4,000 years ago? Of course it is the Ark and not an antiquated craft that some tricky showman has bought for a sou, taken to pieces, dragged up the mountain and reconstructed, for the printed description indicates a model that cannot be found afloat at the present day except in the mudscow fleet of the New York Street Cleaning Department and the navy of the United States, neither of which has yet disposed of any of its antediluvian hulks.

"Well, what are the ungodly going to do about it? There she is, according to the Turkish press, which has no possible reason to go so far back into antiquity if searching merely for something to lie about. It will not do for them to make light of the story, for an Englishman has discovered that the ancient cattle boat is of gopher wood, according to specifications, and the stalls are in accordance with the plans of the British Admiralty, which body is the modern substitute for inspiration in marine affairs. All that Colonel Ingersoll and Professor Adler can hope for is to persuade the public that the newly discovered antique, although an Ark, is not necessarily the handiwork of an amateur ship carpenter named Noah. If arks were the fashion forty-four hundred years ago, why may not dozens of them have drifted from their moorings during the great November freshet of 2516 B.C. and gone ashore on Mount Ararat?

"But whatever they may have to say must be said in a hurry, for an American is reported to have arranged to bring the old tub over here, and argument will stand a poor chance against eyesight. If she is three hundred cubits long, according to contract, it may be quite a job to get her from the top of Mount Ararat to the Mediterranean, but a nation that has seriously thought of a ship railway across Central America cannot doubt that the ark can be brought to deep water. If no American engineers of sufficient ability are on the ground, the purchasers need only send to France for Jules Verne. All but three of her compartments are said to be full of ice, which, at present prices, ought to pay for the expenses of bringing her over here.

"When she reaches American waters, however, the Navy Department ought to purchase her at once, for the world's greatest republic ought to have at least one ship that will not rot as soon as it leaves a navy yard. Her absorption by the government would not prevent the public from getting bits of her relics, even timber enough to make walking canes, pulpit chairs, and pool boxes for all who care to buy; for when our Naval Department does "improve" a vessel, it gets rid of so much of the original material that, in the case of the ark, Noah would not know his staunch old family scow if he saw it."

Three days later (August 13, 1883) the New York *World* published this article:

"Considerable competition has recently been shown by the discoverers of ancient manuscripts and the finders of ancient relics. The latter have suddenly come to the front by the discovery of Noah's Ark in that part of the Armenian plateau still known as Mount Ararat.

"The find was made by a party of Russian engineers [understandable mistake as many people think the mountain is in Russia] who were surveying a glacier. An extraordinary spell of hot weather had melted away a great portion of the Araxes glacier, and they were surprised to see sticking out of the ice what at first appeared to be the crude facade of an ancient dwelling. On closer examination it was found to be composed of longitudinal layers of gopher wood, supported by immense frames, still in a remarkable state of preservation.

"Assistance having been summoned from Nakhchevan, the work of uncovering the find was commenced under the most extraordinary difficulties and in a week's time, the indefatigable explorers had uncovered a section of what they claim to be Noah's ark as it bore evidence of having been used as a boat.

"At this point archaeology could afford to rest at any ordinary period of the world, and we should expect the luckiest finders to form a syndicate and open a bazaar for the sale of relics.

"But in our day antiquarian industry takes another turn. It isn't looking for merchandise so much as to the testimony. We must not forget that the planting of the Cardiff Giant was not so much to make money as to establish the missing link.

"The Noah's Ark syndicate are only following the tactics of the antiquary who recently offered to sell an original manuscript of the Mosaic Law, signed by Moses, to the British Museum.

"They are trying to correct the record with facts.

"With these principles in view, the reader must not be surprised to learn by the latest dispatches from our representative, Mr. Benjamin, who is not going to Persia for nothing, that the engineers have broken through the third compartment of the ark, and in the true spirit of the age have discovered the original log kept by Noah and his sons.

"Startling as this announcement is, it is backed up by the documents which must stand for what they are worth without any comment of ours. Philology, ethnology, and archaeology must fight it out for themselves. A newspaper can only narrate the occurrence."

If there is any doubt as to how much attention the reported discovery received, one only has to scan other papers such as the New York *Times* (August 15, 1883), the *Watchtower* (September, 1883), and the British *Pall Mall Gazette* to be convinced of its newsworthiness.

But the *British Prophetic Messenger* of that year contained what may well be the most exact story of the find, quoting as its source the Levant *Herald:*

"We have received from our correspondent in Trebizond news of the return of the Commissioners appointed by the Turkish Government to inquire into the reported destruction of Mosul, Ashak, and Bayazid by avalanches, and to render relief to the distressed villages in the glens of the Ararat ranges, who had suffered so severely from the unusual inclemency of the season.

"The expedition was fortunate in making a discovery that cannot fail to be of interest to the whole civilized world, for among the vastnesses of one of the glens of Mount Ararat, they came upon a gigantic structure of very dark wood, embedded at the foot of one of the glaciers, with one end protruding, and which they believe to be none other than the old Ark in which Noah and his family navigated the waters of the Deluge. The place where the discovery is made is about five days' journey from Trebizond, in the Department of Van, in Armenia, about four leagues from the Persian frontier.

"The villagers of Bayazid, which was situated about a league away, had seen this strange object for nearly six years, but were deterred by a strong superstitious fear of approaching, as there was a rumor, generally believed, that strange voices were heard within it, and it is said that some, more daring than others, who had approached had seen a spirit of fierce aspect gazing out of a hole or door in the upper portion of the structure.

"The Commissioners, accompanied by their personal attendants, proceeded to examine it, the villagers positively refusing even to approach the neighborhood of the glacier in which it was embedded. The way led through a dense forest, and the travelers were obliged to follow the course of a stream, wading sometimes waist high in water which was intensely cold being from the melting glacier.

"At last they were rewarded by the sight of a huge dark mass, protruding twenty or thirty feet from the glacier, on the left side of the ravine. They found it was formed of wood not grown in these elevated districts, not nearer than the hot valleys of the Euphrates, where it is known by the natives as 'izim,' said to be the gopher wood of the Scriptures. It was in a good state of preservation, being painted on the outside with a dark brown pigment, and constructed of great strength.

"It was a good deal broken at the angles from being subjected to somewhat rough usage by the moraine during the slow descent of the glacier from the lofty peaks towering away beyond the head of the valley to a height of over 17,000 feet, a process which, considering the nature of the country and the slow pace at which these snow rivers travel, especially in the higher altitudes, must have required thousands of years. The projected portion seemed about forty or fifty feet in height, but to what length it penetrated into the glacier they could not estimate.

"Effecting an entrance through one of the broken corners, the explorers found it filled for the greater part with ice, the interior being partitioned off into compartments about twelve or fifteen feet high, into three of which only they were able to make their way, owing to the mass of frozen substance with which these were filled, and also because of their fear of the structure collapsing with the overhanging mass of the huge glacier.

"The Commissioners, one of whom was an Englishman, Captain Cascoyne, formerly attached to the British Embassy in this city, and well known as a scientific investigator, are fully confident that it is the Ark of Noah, and they support the position by maintaining that, having been enveloped in snow and frozen, it has been kept in a state of perfect preservation.

"Having rested on one of the peaks of the Ararat range, as described in the Scriptures, the Ark must have lain on soil, for 'the waters covered the whole earth, and the high hills and the mountains were covered.' In these circumstances the snow that ordinarily covers this lofty mountain—for it is 17,230 feet high —would have been all melted by the waters of the flood when Noah grounded on the peak. But as the waters were slowly receding for some five months, and Noah and his family, following the receding waters, gradually made their way to the lowlands, the mountain would of course resume its great height above the sea level, and in consequence, be again covered with snow, which must have once enveloped the Ark as it lay—it may be supposed—on this slope near the summit of the peak. As perpetual snow covers Mount Ararat more than half way down, it is manifest that the Ark must have been kept in a perfect state of preservation, while slowly, during the lapse of four or five thousand years, creeping down, after the manner of the glaciers, into the valley below, though in later ages to discomfort the scoffer and confirm the sure word of revelation."

CHAPTER 5

"And the ark rested in the seventh month, on the seventeenth day of the month upon the mountains of Ararat."

It was this phrase that kept reechoing through my mind while I absentmindedly pulled the key from the hook in the lobby of the Grand Hotel Bahlin in Ankara and squeezed myself hurriedly into the tiny elevator. It was Thursday night, May 26, 1960; and a few hours from now the Turkish government was to issue the final ministerial approval of the Cabinet of Ministers that would allow our entire ark expedition to move into the wild mountainous region of eastern Turkey to search for what they considered to be one of the strangest objects of the much disputed ancient history of the Middle East—Noah's ark.

It had been quite an evening. The growing political crisis in the country seemed to have had a paralyzing effect on the population of the nation's capital, for everywhere things were quiet—too quiet—and an ominous feeling of pending violence hung over the city like a shroud. No one could identify the cause, but everyone sensed the danger. All expedition members were already in bed, and even though it was very late, I recapped the political situation with Eric de Mouny of the BBC while listening to the latest newscast in the hotel lobby. I still remember that after finally retiring to my room, I reached for my diary to record the events of the day. But I was too tired and immediately fell asleep.

It was nearly four o'clock in the morning when a sudden burst of machine-gun fire triggered right underneath my window. I quickly slid out of bed and into my Air Force jumpsuit and rushed out of the room. I dashed down the stairs and peeked through the lobby door to get my first glimpse of the unexpected excitement that had hit the capital. My cameras banged against the wall as I charged out the door and continued on my way to the street, coming face to face with a new revolution. Tanks rattled by and machine-gun nests were guarding every street corner in the downtown area. Everywhere in the city soldiers were positioned at strategic spots. A Turk standing behind me smiled.

"The army has taken over," he chuckled. "This means the end of the government of Adnan Menderes."

His words were indeed prophetic, for three short hours later the new military regime was already in control of the entire country. Adnan Menderes had been taken into custody, while Fatim Rustu Zorlu, Minister of Foreign Affairs, had been apprehended trying to leave the country. I had heard about his arrest through the grinding rumor mill, and it worried me, for Zorlu was the man who had backed our request for permission. His capture and the overthrow of the entire government could mean nothing but disaster for our expedition plans.

It was ironic. Here I was with a fiery revolution all around me, but aside from a few hurried reports for the news syndicate, there wasn't much I could do, for the reasons that had brought me to Turkey were not of a political nature. Far from it.

My 1960 Turkish involvement had begun several months before on that memorable KLM flight from Beirut when the stewardess had handed me the New York *Herald Tribune* containing the news item about the possible discovery of Noah's ark in eastern Turkey.* It had been a full ten years since I had worked on the ark project. The involvement with the Smith expedition of 1949 and the resulting charges from the Russian press bureau *Pravda* and Radio Moscow that we, the American, British, and Dutch members of the group, were working for Western intelligence-gathering organizations had forced me to drop out, for in my profession I could ill afford this stigma. But this newly reported discovery had rekindled my ark fever, and I'd dug into the project without hesitation.

Within days after the newspaper story had hit the world, I was knocking at the door of the office of Dr. Arthur Brandenburger, professor of photogrammetry at the Ohio State University in Columbus.

With his soft Swiss accent and a good-natured smile, he told me as much as he knew concerning the discovery, and from his account and the subsequent conversations I had with Captain Ilhan Durupinar of the Turkish army, the story soon fell into shape.

It had been a freezing cold night in Ankara, Turkey, when Ilhan Durupinar had entered his photogrammetry laboratory on the outskirts of the city. Shoving his way past the heavy oak door to his office, he pulled off his overcoat.

He shivered. His hand reached out and turned on the hall light, and the echoes of his footsteps bounced coldly from wall to wall as he made his way to the negative file in the corner of the laboratory. Almost mechanically he pulled out a new set of unexamined stereoplates from the files—and sighed as he looked at them.

"Negatives," he mumbled to himself, dreading another day's dreary routine of examining nothing but lines and ridges. "Always negatives." He closed the drawer with an absentminded gesture as he walked over to the Wild A-7 Stereoplanograph to

---

*See Chapter 1

get his first look at the new negs. Slowly he cranked the machine until the plates came into focus. He stopped and lit a cigarette. It had been a rough night. He rubbed his eyes and looked again.

Carefully he scanned the various sections of the photograph and then suddenly stopped. He adjusted the A-7 and then looked again! Yes, there it was! No mistake about it! There, at an approximate height of 6,000 feet high in the Ararat mountains, his negatives disclosed the presence of a strange, unexpected ship-like object, alone and unattended and seemingly caught in a stream of solidified lava. He turned around and called the colonel in charge who had just entered the laboratory. Both men crowded close to the viewer as they stared at the extraordinary find.

The colonel's initial cynicism quickly changed to marked excitement.

"It can't be," he began to stammer. "Yet it looks like a ship!" Within minutes the exhilaration of the two men spread throughout the laboratory. One by one the officers stopped by and walked up to the viewer of the stereoplanograph and gazed in astonishment at the unknown object. One by one they left, shaking their heads and wondering.

The colonel took Ilhan Durupinar by the arm and walked with him to one of the windows.

"Out of exactly which batch of negatives did you pull this one, captain?" he asked. "Was it the NATO survey?"

Captain Durupinar nodded.

"Yes, sir. They belong to those taken over the Ararat region for the latest NATO job."

"You mean the pictures taken by Major Kurtis last summer?"

"Yes, sir."

"Captain," the colonel asked, "you're not a Christian, are you?"

"No, sir," the Moslem captain replied.

"Well," the colonel continued, with a voice shaken by intense emotion, "do you have any idea what you have just been looking at?"

"A rock formation, Colonel?"

The colonel sat down and let his head rest on his fisted hand.

"It's the ark, Durupinar," he said softly. "You have just discovered Noah's ark on the place where it finally settled thousands of years ago. Durupinar, you may well have made the discovery of the century, for to both Moslems and Christians alike, Noah was the great prophet who on God's commandment survived the Great Flood that punished the world. And he survived it in a ship. *That* ship!" He pointed to the negative on the A-7.

That night, Captain Ilhan Durupinar went home not realizing that his discovery was to create an immense disturbance among archaeologists and scientists for years to come. Shaking the rain off his coat, he entered his house. It was cold and dark outside, but indoors a brightly burning fireplace greeted him. It was the evening of September 23, 1959, and he, Ilhan Durupinar, had just launched a new scientific controversy.

"Have you had a chance to check the negatives?" I asked Professor Brandenburger after he had briefed me on the meager details at his disposal. "Have you formed an opinion as to its significance?"

He leaned back in his chair and pointed at the two negatives on his desk.

"I have studied them," he answered before I had even finished. "I have no doubt at all that this object is a ship. In my entire career I have never seen an object like this on a stereo photo. Not only that, but all the calculations we have thus far been able to make support this. Even the approximate length of the object fits. Based on our measurements, it is about 150 meters, and that is also supposed to have been the length of the Biblical ark." He paused before making his final statement.

"I have no doubt about the importance of this find," he concluded. "The sooner we get a field party going the better I will like it."

Listening to him, I had already made up my mind as to what to do.

"I'm planning an expedition to the site to investigate this object, doctor. Will you join me?"

He slapped me on the shoulder while his other hand stubbed out his smoldering cigar butt.

"Count on me, Rene," he answered, smiling while he talked. "Work it out, get others to join us, and let's go!"

Within minutes, a hurried phone call to the magazine editors of *Munich Illustrated* in Germany and to Tom Blau of *Camera Press Limited* in London gave me the necessary backing to launch an expedition. My sources were willing to furnish $25,000 for my efforts, with more to come if needed. While Professor Brandenburger returned to his classroom, I headed for Greensboro, North Carolina, to interview Dr. Aaron J. Smith, the man with whom I had been associated in the 1949 expedition.

In the days immediately following my meeting with Brandenburger, I stopped by the office of George Vandeman, an old friend in Washington, and the moment I walked in I knew something was stirring.

"I want to let you in on a secret," he confided to me after our first friendly greeting. "There's been a story about a possible discovery of Noah's ark in the papers, and I want to go and investigate it. Professor Brandenburger is going with me!"

"Have you asked him yet?" I blurted out.

"No, not yet, but I intend to see him tomorrow."

"That won't be necessary now," I interjected. "I just came from him and already signed him up for an expedition."

With both of us wanting to investigate the same object, there was no reason why we should not combine our efforts, and we soon agreed to a merger with each side bringing experts to form a complete scientific team. With an abundance of enthusiasm and internal friction, plans were finalized for the 1960 expedition. However, once the word was out that a concerted attempt would be made to locate the actual ark, hardly any time elapsed before offers of support were received from both financial wizards and educated crooks. Hurried consultations with a group of New York financiers culminated in the forming of a corporation that would handle the ark affairs with a total budget of up to one million dollars.

Vandeman and I attended the first meeting of the financial group on Park Avenue, New York. Sitting there, I felt like a financially undernourished pauper with my insignificant $25,000 commitment in my pocket, for they were talking money, *big* money!

The spokesman* of the Pan Asia Banking Corporation, announced that he was planning to put $1,000,000 into the project, and with it he presented us with a breakdown as to how the money would be spent:

"We want to buy a few DC-3 airplanes so that the expedition will have its own transportation within Turkey. We want to ship bulldozers to the foot of the mountain to cut our own landing strip and to facilitate things for expedition members and their guests; we intend to buy a Liberty ship and leave it as a floating hotel in the Mediterranean. We will also of course need a number of Jeeps, buses, helicopters, and our own radio station. A complete film crew will have to be brought in, because we intend to make this the greatest expedition of all times."

In addition, the avenues to the right people in Turkey had already been arranged, but it was an invited guest to the meeting, the Turkish Press Bureau representative, who showed us the Ottoman way of doing things.

When we requested his advice, he agreed to give all the help and leads needed, with the provision that we would pay for each contact supplied to us, with half of the money going to him and the other half to the individuals in Turkey. Furthermore, an undetermined amount of money was to be paid to him for each day one of the contacts was actively involved in help-

---

*Name deleted to avoid embarrassment.

ing us find our way through the maze of Turkish red tape.

Our objections barely registered. The chairman tried to soften the blow.

"If you've got problems," he smiled disarmingly, "don't worry. 'Gene' [Eugene Black, president of the World Bank] owes me a favor. If needed, we can call on him! Also, don't forget, Turkey just got a loan of $359 million through us, so they'll cooperate even on a strict courtesy basis." Names of Turkish cabinet members bounced from wall to wall, leaving the impression that nothing would hinder the progress of the expedition.

With the oral financial backing of the newly formed group and supplied with ample introductions to high-ranking members of the Turkish government, George Vandeman, Don Loveridge, one of our financiers, and I rushed to Ankara to commence negotiations with the cabinet for the expedition permit. At the same time, a public relations firm in New York set the wheels in motion to start earning their promised $3,000 per month plus expenses as authorized by the chairman in order to promote the efforts of the new expedition.

Things were rough at first, but thanks to sheer bluff and luck, we finally scaled the obstacles and received a promise of total cooperation.

It was the director of the Department of Archaeology who raised the first serious objection to our plans.

While we were visiting him in his office in Ankara, Dr. Kamil Su pulled out a clipping of the Turkish magazine *Hyatt*.

Pinning it on the wall, he looked at it with a scrutinizing stare. Then he called us over.

"Now," he questioned, "where is your ark? Can you show it to me?" And with that he sat down in his chair and waited.

The three of us stood up and walked over to the wall. Could it be that he was serious? Did he actually expect to find a picture of "the object" on *that* magazine clipping?

"Well?" he asked impatiently. "Where is it? Didn't you just

get through telling me that *Hyatt* had also published the aerial photograph, and did I not show you the page on which this picture is supposed to be?"

Don was the first to recover his voice.

"Dr. Su," he said hesitantly, but kindly, "whoever gave you that picture does not want you to know the truth. *You have only the top half.* They have cut the picture in two and given you the section which shows nothing but the bare mountainside."

Dr. Kamil Su stared at us, his mouth agape. His own people had tried to fool him deliberately to avoid the chance of his issuing a permit to investigate the object.

Don then pulled the complete *Hyatt* clipping from his briefcase and handed it to him. Kamil Su smiled sheepishly.

"Probably the work of one of my Moslem employees." His face sour, he dismissed the issue with a shrug of his shoulders. "With a mixed staff, one never knows."

Immediately the archaeologist in him awakened.

"I'll give you whatever help I can in view of this new development," he promised. "You can have the exclusive rights to the area for a period of two months."

With that official obstacle behind us, our next target was Zorlu, minister of foreign affairs. Since we were foreigners wanting to work in the Turkish military zone, his permission was needed. We had been to the office before and had got nowhere. But this time we succeeded in gaining admittance.

The meeting that followed resulted in another promise of unreserved cooperation. It seemed that the expedition was finally on its way!

From the first moment the promise of permission was received, and we had returned to the United States, internal friction began to tear the organization apart. The individuals responsible for bringing in the New York financiers now began to run the group, and they might have succeeded in enlisting our full support had it not been for the $25,000 request.

It came via George Vandeman, directed to Don Loveridge.

"The New York financiers have asked me to have you deposit $25,000 into the expedition fund," he relayed, "so they can use this to work on the plans for the expedition while their $1,000,000 is being redeemed from stocks and bonds."

Don had already advanced all the money used thus far and was not at all enthusiastic about this new development.

"Give me twenty-four hours," he reacted, "and we'll work it out."

And while I sat in Don's living room, he pulled out his private phone list and began dialing. Within hours, a flurry of calls came pouring in, reporting that some of the interested backers were nearly bankrupt, and others with whom we were dealing had been suspected of fraud and embezzlement. It appeared that the ark of Father Noah was to become the target of some dubious financial schemes. Another phone call heightened our growing suspicions. Never, we were informed, had these financiers lent the Turkish government $359 million! If Turkish Foreign Minister Zorlu had known of this, he could have branded us impostors, but Turkey was facing bankruptcy itself and had borrowed so many millions from so many groups that Zorlu just could not keep track of it.

Needless to say, the million-dollar expedition was dead. The first "big money" meeting had been held on January 13, but by February 12, exactly one month later, it had fizzled. We were back where we started, planning a small manageable expedition, without the million dollars and without Liberty ships or DC-3's. Much time had been lost, but our integrity, we hoped, had been saved.

It was a report from Dr. Brandenburger that reestablished our faith and enthusiasm in the project.

After careful study of the stereo negatives, he wrote,

"I am pleased to inform you that we have finished our measurements. The results are shown on the maps I have enclosed.

These measurements show that the petrified ship has a length of 500 feet, a width of 160 feet, and reaches a height of 20 feet in some places. The inclination of the ship amounts to 11½ degrees. The documents show a topographic map in the scale of 1:1500, 16 cross sections, 2 longitudinal sections and a perspective of the ship.

"In carrying out these measurements with the Wild A-7, the impression that the finding must be a petrified ship was further substantiated."

Don, George, and I breathed a sigh of relief. The expedition was back on the trail. However, we had not counted on the sudden revolution that was to hit us at the moment when we were to receive our final permit.

So here we were—immobilized by a government coup. With all of the cabinet members imprisoned and the various government departments immobilized due to lack of leadership, we had no alternative but to wait. Yet through a friendship I developed with Colonel Turkesh, a member of the Revolutionary Committee of National Unity, I gained access to General Gursel, the new head of state. Together with him and Colonel Alatli, another member of the committee, we discussed the expedition's fate. As a result one of the first decisions made by the Committee of National Unity was to permit us to enter the military zone.

Our days were crowded with solving logistical problems, traveling to Erzurum, and finally to Dogubayazit, a sleepy headquarters town of the Turkish Third Army, where we were assigned our army escort consisting of Major Baykal and fifteen foot soldiers. Baykal, a cavalry officer, abhored any other mode of transportation; consequently, we were borne by six of the meanest-looking horses into the rugged mountain terrain. Following Baykal, we ventured into the saddle region between Ararat and Tenderick, about twenty miles from the Iranian border.

My diary, dated June 6, 1960, recalls the events:

"It was 7:45 in the morning, when the major, who had galloped ahead of the first group, raised his arm and stopped the column on a gentle mountain slope. Tired and saddle sore, we dismounted. It hadn't been a long ride—a few hours at the most —but everyone welcomed the change. It was quite a group, for much had happened since George and I had gotten together.

"Here we were, a group of men representing a variety of professions. There was Professor Arthur J. Brandenburger, one of the world's foremost experts in photogrammetry and aerial photography; Captain Ilhan Durupinar, expert cartographer; Wilbur A. Bishop, self-made millionaire and one of the financiers of the expedition; George Vandeman, Protestant minister; Hal J. Thomsen, research assistant; and Dr. S. H. Horn, well respected archaeologist." (Dr. Horn did not share the enthusiasm of the others. He had little interest and still less faith in the ark project, and had accompanied the group reluctantly, after much urging.)

"Major Baykal wandered away from us and looked at his maps. Then he turned and let his eyes scan the surrounding landscape. A feeling of disgust and dismay came over us, for no one felt this interruption was justified.

"Suddenly the major shouted, 'There she is, men—there she is!' "

"Gone was all the disgust! We had expected to reach a volcanic area; in fact, all our expectations had been built on the statements of Durupinar and Professor Brandenburger who had said that the aerial photographs indicated that the object rested in a stream of lava. Yet, here we were amidst jagged mountains and gentle sloping valleys—and this was it?

"We looked in the direction he pointed, and there, across a greenish-brown valley lay the perfect image of a ship, nestled among the rocks. It certainly could not be a case of mistaken identity. It looked like a ship; yet somehow it didn't fit the photographic study. Could this actually be the ark? All reports

I had been studying these past years dealt with the ark being on one of the peaks of the mountain of Ararat, but this location was not only a great distance from the top, but it didn't fit the mental image of what a petrified ship caught in a lava stream should look like. The thoughts that entered my head doubtless occupied the others, for during several minutes not a word was said.

"I got my cameras in action and started shooting.

"'Rene, what do you think of it?' George called out. 'It's so different from what I expected to find.' Keen disappointment showed on his face. Nervously he fingered his silvery hair. 'This doesn't seem to be it, and yet it fits the picture. It must be the same object.'

"Professors Horn and Brandenburger joined us.

"'Looks like a ship,' Brandenburger commented.

"'Yes, but where's the lava stream?' interrupted Hal Thomsen.

"Climbing over rocks, crawling through crevasses and stumbling most of the way, we reached the earthen wall that had been identified on the aerial photograph as the probable side of the ship.

"Out of breath, I crawled over the side and entered the object. At last! Gone was all the dreaming; finished was all the planning. We had reached the object, and the investigation could commence. I turned and watched the other expedition members climb 'aboard.' In depressing silence, all stood aghast at the difference between expectation and reality. While Brandenburger and Durupinar unpacked their field equipment, Dr. Horn scouted for the right spot for the first dig. With hand tools hurriedly borrowed from curious natives in a near village, the first trench was dug. The bits of dirt and stone that were thrown in our direction bore no resemblance to the expected petrified beams we had anticipated.

"The dark gathering clouds that had been with us in Dogubayazit now began to cover the mountainside, reaching all the way to the summit of Greater Ararat, obscuring its shiny face from the intruders.

"Time passed slowly, but no discoveries were made. Dr. Horn pointed out that we might be at the wrong spot.

" 'If these long heaps of dirt are formed this way because of the presence of an actual ship underneath,' he reasoned, 'then we should have come to it by this time. Nothing of any archaeological value has been discovered thus far. It doesn't seem right—'

"A second trench was decided upon; this time digging from the inside toward the outside, but all this did was increase the unhappiness of the team. The 15-foot high side revealed nothing."

The next day's excavation probe did not reveal much more; however, the technique that followed was drastically different.

"Let's try dynamite!" Wilbur Bishop had suggested shortly before terminating the first day's probe, and the following day this was to be the predominant tactic. Needless to say, this was a decidedly unorthodox method for archaeological research, and the team's archaeologist strongly opposed this desperate maneuver. Conventional methods of excavation were adhered to until 11:45 a.m. To do a thorough job, a shaft should have been dug in the center of the object, while two trenches, one crosswise, another lengthwise, should also have been made. The lack of an actual excavation permit did not allow us to follow that course of action; therefore, at the right side of the bow, the second hole was enlarged and nine sticks of dynamite were inserted. One fuse and 1½ minutes later, the sticks of 1935-vintage explosives blackened the dirt with a tremendous explosion. Again, all that was found was dirt, rocks, and more dirt. No ark.

It was 12:12 p.m., June 7, 1960, when the excavation officially ended.

"Let's go home, folks," George Vandeman suggested after he had climbed out of the latest hole. "It's finished."

It was a discouraged and sorrowful heap of humanity that

walked down the slope that day, back to the spot where the horses waited. Two days later we were back in Ankara where the expedition was pronounced finished, and the following news release was issued to the assembled journalists:

"SCIENTIFIC TEAM INVESTIGATES BOAT-SHAPED OBJECT IN EASTERN TURKEY"

"With the full permission of the new government, an investigative team sent to eastern Turkey by the Archaeological Research Foundation of Washington, D.C., has just returned to Ankara after completing its study of a large boat-shaped object that appeared in an aerial photograph made by the Turkish army.

"The team under the leadership of Mr. George Vandeman, located the object twenty miles south of Mount Ararat near the Iranian border. Captain Ilhan Durupinar of the Turkish cartographic service, who originally discovered the peculiar shape in the aerial photograph, was a member of the group.

"Dr. Brandenburger, photogrammetry expert of the Ohio State University, foremost member of the team, stated, 'Our measurements in the field verify our laboratory findings. In my opinion further study of this peculiar symmetrical phenomenon should be made by an expert in tectonics.'

"The team found a landslide on a gentle mountain slope. Earthen walls within the slide were apparently pushed into the shape of a boat. There were no visible archaeological remains.

"Mr. Vandeman concluded that 'the mission was scientifically successful. We located the site and made our measurements. We identified the supposed object and ascertained to our satisfaction that it was a freak of nature and not man-made. It is of no further interest to us, so we shall not send an archaeological expedition into the area.'"

Officially it was all over, but the group was divided as to whether we should have gone on. In a "Confidential Report" to backers and members of the expedition, George Vandeman admitted: "It is possible, however, that our conclusions at the time were more negative than they should have been. Some in the group are not convinced that we have fully explored the possibility that something may be buried beneath the site that may have caused that portion of the earth to remain so symmetrical and boatlike a formation. Dr. Brandenburger writes me under date of June 24, (1960):

"'Meanwhile I have received my developed colored slides of the ship-shaped formation, and I still must say it is an amazing feature. In any case it will be very difficult to explain its existence from the geological standpoint.

"'I showed the slides to some of my friends, and they were of the same opinion. It is doubtless a mystery, and I come always more to the conclusion that our official statement to the press was too negative. The interpretation of the formation is of utmost difficulty, and I am not anymore so sure that, from a serious scientific standpoint, a sole surface archaeological investigation of only two days entitles us to state that the formation is not the ark.'"

But it was all finished; the dream of a million-dollar expedition was all over. In a series of unsuccessful attempts, it had been just another try to find the most celebrated artifact of ancient history.

It failed, but the search continued.

CHAPTER 6

It must have caused a chuckle or two in a certain household in Bordeaux, France, when the 1960 Archaeological Research Foundation expedition returned to Ankara beaten and empty-handed.

I can just imagine Fernand Navarra smiling while reaching for an aged hunk of blackened wood on a display table and saying to his son, "You know, Raphael, I knew they'd come back this way. You knew it too, didn't you? Where they were searching, it simply couldn't have been the ark, for only we know where it is, and they're way off!"

I can almost see the piteous glances of understanding that flashed between them when the French television newscasters announced the end of the first Ararat expedition launched by the ARF. But then, if Fernand Navarra, French demolition expert, had reacted in that manner, he must have felt that he had adequate reasons to show pity, for he had climbed Mount Ararat three different times during the early fifties, and the results of his last effort had given him sufficient basis to doubt the outcome of ARF's first encounter with the holy mountain.

For Navarra the search for Noah's ark had begun many years before, in 1937, when he was serving his stint in the French army in the Middle East. One day while stationed in the Damascus area, he and an Armenian friend named Alim began an ascent of Mount Hermon. At an elevation of approximately 8,000 feet, Alim begged to be left behind, and Fernand stubbornly continued his climb alone to the top of the 10,000-foot mountain. It was on the downward trail later that day that Alim rejoined him and told his young companion about his background and his fondest dream.

"As a youngster I lived on a small island in the middle of Lake Van in Armenia," he hesitantly confided to Fernand; "but I still remember going to see my aging grandfather in Bayazit before we left there to come to Syria. He lived at the foot of Mount Ararat." Alim paused for a moment, staring up at the lofty heights of Hermon. Navarra's interest held, fortunately so, for Alim continued his tale, telling his French friend that his grandfather had assured him that the story of Noah's ark was not a mere fable of the Armenians but that the ancient ship was still resting somewhere on the mountain waiting to be discovered.

Only old age, his grandfather had declared, had prevented him from searching for the ship, and he was now counting on his grandson to go one day and find the holy ark.

"He wants me to, but I can't," Alim sadly admitted, comparing his body to the excellent physique of the fascinated young soldier. "I tire too easily. But how about *you* trying it?"

Alim's story awakened the adventurer in Fernand, but two years later, booming cannons and flashing bayonets introduced the agony of the second world war, and dreams of Noah's ark were choked in infancy.

In the postwar period conditions in Europe were such that traveling was very difficult, and it was not until the summer of 1952, roughly fifteen years after his hasty introduction to the secret of the ark, that Fernand Navarra, now married and the father of three sons, managed to find the time to fulfill his companion's dream and climb Mount Ararat.

The stories as to how the 1952 expedition got its initial start differ to some extent, depending upon which version supersedes the others. Navarra maintains that he furnished the financial backing and led the group to the snowy peaks of Armenia. However, a careful check of the Bordeaux newspaper *Sud Ouest* revealed a story in one of its 1952 issues naming *Jeane de Riquer,* a man whom Navarra claimed was one of *his* expedition members, as the leader of the expedition. Fernand Navarra barely received a one-line mention.

No matter who led out, Navarra did go in 1952 and claimed he discovered a ship's hull.

It was two o'clock in the afternoon of August 17, at an elevation of approximately 14,000 feet, when the amateur explorers noticed an unusual dark patch within the ice, having sharp, well-defined outlines.

Quoting Navarra, "Fascinated and intrigued, . . . we began straightway to trace out its shape, mapping out its limit foot by foot; two progressively incurving lines were revealed which were clearly defined for a distance of three hundred cubits before meeting in the heart of the glacier. The shape was unmistakably that of a ship's hull: on either side the edges of the patch curved like the gunwales of a great boat. As for the central part, it merged into a black mass the details of which were not discernible."[1]

Thoughtfully commenting on this first sighting at a later date in his book *J'ai Trouve l'Arche de Noe* (I Found Noah's Ark), Navarra enlarged on the emotional reaction that struck him at that moment:

"I have never been subject to visions; I am perfectly clear-headed, and I can call upon a faculty not possessed by crazy people: good sense.

"At this altitude, in this wilderness of ice, what could it be? The ruins of a structure, a church, a refuge, or house . . . ? The wreck of a plane? Even in the greatest periods of aviation, beams of this size would never be used for an air frame. The evidence must be acknowledged; the remains are those of the Ark, if only because it cannot be anything else."[2]

Lack of proper excavating equipment plus extreme cold forced Navarra and his fellow adventurers to return to Europe. A short year later, however, he was back on an excursion he calls his "second expedition," even though this time he climbed the mountain accompanied only by a Turkish photographer. But due to illness he was forced to retreat down the mountainside before reaching the target site. It was not until the summer of 1955 that he left France to make his third and final attempt, accompanied by his wife and three sons aged nine, eleven, and thirteen.

With Raphael, his eleven-year-old boy, as his only climbing companion (the others remained in a small hotel at the foot of the mountain), the "third expedition" finally reached the bleak and frozen spot of his 1952 discovery. But everything looked so different! The seasons had reaped their harvest on the mountain, and after probing and digging in sub-zero temperature with blizzards and rockslides to contend with, he felt he had to quit. Disappointment closed in on the tired mountaineers—and then it happened!

"Under the pierced ice core, water appeared, and in the water appeared the extremity of a dark beam. Not believing my eyes," he wrote in February, 1965, "I touched it, dug my nails into it. But I was not dreaming. I was really touching a piece of wood —wood that had been worked, and not the trunk of a tree. I felt a lump in my throat. I wanted to cry, to kneel right there and thank God to have allowed me this success.

"I tried to loosen the piece of wood in its entirety, but could not, in spite of having widened the hole. It must have been a very long beam. Was it still fastened to another part of the ship's frame? I settled for a piece 5 feet long, which was showing, and cut it following the grain. Out of the water its weight surprised me. This wood had been worked; it was only too evident. Its state of preservation was unbelievable. Was it due to the pitch?

"I took a first set of pictures and movies, then returned to the foot of the ladder. There I fastened the piece of the ark to the rope and left it below in order to let Raphael have the joy of bringing it up himself."[3]

Too excited to wait until his return to France for a scientific identification of the piece of wood, he briefly stopped at the Cairo Museum in Egypt, where an available expert estimated the sample to be between 4,000 and 6,000 years old.

With the subsequent publication of a book relating his adventures on the mountain and his discovery of the actual ark of Noah—for he had indeed found the remnants of the ship, of that he had no doubt—he embarked on a lecture tour and was soon recognized in Europe as a modern discoverer of Noah's ark. To reenforce his claim as *the* discoverer, he assembled an impressive documentation, showing that the wood could certainly have belonged to the era of the Deluge.

Tests conducted by the Institute Forestal in Madrid, the Centre de Technique de Bois in Paris, and the Institute Prehistoire de L'Universite Bordeaux (France) more than supported his initial enthusiasm. Their findings, based on the degree of lignite formation in the wood samples, gain in density, cell modification and the degree of fossilization of the wood, indicated that the wood is of "great antiquity" (Bordeaux). The estimate from the laboratory at Madrid was even more encouraging. It placed the age at approximately 5,000 years. Not to be outdone by their colleagues, the scientists of the Centre de Technique de Bois in Paris quoted 4,484 years as the age of the recovered beam.

It is important to remember that these dates are really only *estimates,* based on assumptions and opinions, utilizing generally accepted techniques.

The first indications I received concerning Fernand Navarra's true feelings about his wood came to me via the Smith files. They yielded valuable clues to Navarra's find, for several letters were exchanged between the two researchers in 1959, showing that

Navarra never doubted for one moment that he was the discoverer of the real artifact, even though others might think differently.

Unreservedly, he stated on January 17, 1959: "In 1953 I ascertained that the ark certainly existed. I approached it to within 60 meters. . . . In 1955, in the company of my son Raphael, I had the good fortune to get as close as possibly 1.50 meters.

"I shall certainly set out again with my son," he promised, "in order to bring back all or part, more or less, or at least sufficiently to reconstitute the ark. This would be the object or goal of the next expedition."

Having worked with Smith in his early research years, I can well imagine that he must have been thrilled at the chance to help Navarra determine the exact identification and effect eventual recovery of the artifact. Even though the files do not contain a copy of an answer to the French discoverer, Navarra's reply to Smith, dated March 6, 1959, indicated that Smith had offered assistance. However, this letter revealed much more. Proud of his success, he shared with Smith the news that even a carbon-14 dating test supported his faith in the identity of the wood sample.

This he should never have done.

"I wish to say to you," he wrote, "that the wood of the ark was subjected to the test of carbon-14 *which gives it the age of 4,484 years.* My aim is to return to Ararat for the purpose of ascertaining further information about the ark." By interjecting the carbon-14 test into the discussion, together with a specific age, he introduced an element of such striking coincidence that his claim becomes suspect. In the foreword to his book written after his third expedition in 1955, Navarra stated that "Biblical chronology places the Flood 1,656 years after man was created, or 2,528 years B.C., about 4,484 years ago." Thus by matching this year *exactly* with a carbon-14 dating result, his claim becomes extremely suspect. Informed Bible students make no claims for the year 4,484 as a definite time period, nor do scientists take a carbon-14 reading as an absolute certainty.

When this correspondence took place, the new dating method of carbon-14 was a mere eleven years old, and had been in existence only seven years when Navarra's wood was tested. When the method was first developed by Dr. Willard F. Libby in 1948, it showed promise of becoming a valuable research tool in determining approximate dates and events in the chronology of mankind. The dating method is based on the fact that radioactive carbon found in materials which were once living organisms can be used to determine the age of the now dead organism. Knowing the rate of disintegration of the carbon-14 atoms, it is understood that one half of them will disintegrate in a period of about 5,600 years. Thus the tests attempt to calculate the elapsed time since the organism died by means of measuring the "half-life" figure and the rate at which the remaining atoms are disintegrating. Never, however, has the inventor, Dr. Libby, claimed to be able to produce absolute and accurate dates by using this technique. The years arrived at are always given with a variant of 3 to 5 percent plus or minus, and even then the method is based on two questionable assumptions which Dr. Libby duly recognizes.

The first assumption is that for the last 20,000 to 30,000 years the amount of cosmic radiation reaching the atmosphere surrounding our planet has remained constant; the other is that the quantity of water in the oceans has not measurably changed during history. Actually, only a minor portion of the radiocarbon created by the cosmic rays is absorbed by plants and animals. A still smaller part is present in the atmosphere, and the largest share is absorbed by the oceans. Experience, however, has established the fact that the carbon-14 method as a scientific tool provides only a guideline.

Navarra's introduction of the year 4,484 as the date of the wood has overtones of having been contrived with a preconceived date in mind. For, translated into English, his carbon-14 report—a copy without letterhead, scientific credentials of the examiner or of the institution where the testing was performed, or the date when it was done—states the following:

"To recapitulate, permit me to say that I am very happy and pleased to say that the age of the wood, by the process 'radiocarbon' would be 4,484 years. This age accords with the chronology of the Bible as shown in the following manner:

Date of the Flood before Christ	2,472
Date on which the experiment on the wood was performed after Christ	1,955
Number of years from the Flood to 1955	4,427
Number of years when the wood was cut before the Flood	57
Total age of the wood as discovered by 'radiocarbon'	4,484

signed,

Carleton Yerex"

If this is an official dating, then it was not borne out in the correspondence; and when Navarra was asked during a recent interview about the Yerex dating, he could not recall the details. My question concerning the whereabouts and origin of this official dating report went unanswered. Whether he did know and his answer was not translated through his son Raphael is something of which I was not made aware, but his reaction certainly increased the element of doubt.

Since Aaron Smith had only an uncertified copy of the Yerex report, Navarra still maintained his claim as the true discoverer of the ark. Therefore when the Archaeological Research Foundation prepared to make another attempt to locate the artifact during the summer of 1962, feelers were sent out to Navarra to join ARF in order that he might share the location of his find with a group of modern adventurers.

Navarra refused to go. The mountain lay quiet until 1964, when a new team of nearly twenty explorers participated in the now frantic search, but again no results were booked.

It was not until 1967, several expeditions later, that serious negotiations were started to interest Fernand Navarra to join the ARF effort. The late Bud Crawford—who was later coleader of the ill-fated 1970 expedition and who scaled Mount Ararat seven times—conducted informal discussions with Navarra. These efforts were finalized in the following communication:

"I am in agreement with you," Navarra wrote to Crawford on June 6, 1967. "I rest no more until it has been realized. I will be at your disposal the early days of July.

"For my security, these essential clauses will be necessary:

"(1) Return to me a guarantee of $20,000.

"(2) Assure me a place on the expedition.

"(3) Permission to write a book about the expedition.

"(4) A percentage of the motion picture film of the expedition."

Bud vividly related these negotiations for me while we were bunking together in the Dilson Hotel in Istanbul during the summer of 1970. He insisted we tape most of the evening's long interviews, often probing his mind for the minutest details, as if sensing his approaching death. From our discussion I gained the unavoidable impression that the expedition for that year (1967) had been planned around the cooperation of Navarra. But Navarra backed off, because the package agreement had not been approved by the foundation. Now, with the expedition unsuccessful in its mission on the mountain, something desperate was in order.

Hoping that a new offer, this time higher, might be worked out, another attempt to assure Navarra's cooperation was made.

"Vandeman [the leader of the team] left and flew right to Biarritz, France, where Navarra was working when we were on the mountain," Bud revealed, "but Navarra's reaction had been the usual.

"Navarra was too busy this time and had been very cool, surprisingly, in view of the fact that George Vandeman [in his function as President of ARF] had offered him $40,000 for himself and $10,000 for his son Raphael *for one day,* just to lead us directly to the spot."

But again—no result.

On the surface it seemed unbelievable that a man would turn down such an offer, yet he had his reasons.

He had spent thousands of dollars on his ark research between 1952 and 1966, and even though his books had increased both his income and his popularity, an unexpected business complication threatened to sabotage it all.

Commented George Vandeman after his desperate trip to Biarritz: "I met and talked with Navarra and discovered that he had suffered near bankruptcy during the summer. It was this that led him previously to ask us for $20,000. He faced nearly $50,000 in unpaid bills, and he was simply hoping to recoup some of it by sharing what he felt was valuable to us. In the meantime, the government had helped him out of the problem and loaned him sufficient funds to finish a demolition job near Biarritz, France, one hundred miles south of Bordeaux. The job must be done by August 31 in order to qualify for these government funds. August 31 was only eight days away, and his job was far from finished."

Another member of ARF went a step further in speaking about the January, 1967, meeting of Navarra with his organization. Said he: "What actually happened was—and I have to go by memory now—Navarra had this wrecking outfit, and he was about to go under, and he needed that much to pull himself out, to keep from going bankrupt. This was the idea for requesting this much in order to get his cooperation."

Since the meeting he mentioned had occurred prior to the 1967 expedition, I threw in a figure I had encountered before, wondering whether it might reveal additional information.

"The $120,000, you mean?" I asked.

"Yes, I think so. I don't know what they compromised at, but even that didn't work out. We didn't go that route. We didn't approve it and didn't take part in that kind of thing. We were just trying to find out what it would take."

But hopeful promises of possible private assistance must have been offered to Navarra at that meeting, for three months later Bud again contacted Navarra and concluded his letter with the wish that a certain member of the board would be able to help him in "obtaining the $120,000 loan that you desire for your business."

But nothing had come of this, and Navarra was certainly not prepared to risk his business on mere *promises* of either $50,000 or $20,000.

However, he was, and still is, a businessman, and another try was made in 1968 when R. E. Crawford, at that time a board member of the almost defunct ARF, met with Navarra in Paris to work out a new arrangement. On July 24, 1968, the final outcome was written in contract form, and it was almost bad enough to transfer the three American members of the proposed four-man expedition to the poorhouse.

Among other stipulations, it provided that the three U.S. members of the group would pay Navarra—in the case artifacts were discovered on the '68 expedition—30 per cent of their net income derived from magazine articles, lectures, and other activities *for a period of nine years,* while the French member of the team would be entitled to keep all revenue of his book about the expedition's find to himself. Almost as an afterthought, most assuredly the result of intense deliberation, it was finally agreed that Navarra would donate 10 percent of his book revenue to his American companions.

That same Paris meeting also gave birth to a new organization. Later known as the *Scientific Exploration and Archaeological Research Foundation,* it was formally organized by Ralph E. Crawford. While the aforementioned meeting resulted in organizing a new expedition, this one was not officially known as a SEARCH Foundation probe, even though it was that, for all intent and purposes. It was Navarra's fourth climb, but an unsuccessful one.

Bud Crawford had much to say about this.

"We literally risked our necks," he said. "Rocks were falling all over us. We climbed around that day and went to our camp waiting for Navarra, but he never showed up. [They had left him at the base camp in order to set up another camp at a spot to which Navarra had led Bill Dougal, another expedition member.] "We called and hollered, but no Navarra. We actually picked straws and drew for the job of going out to try and find Navarra. I climbed down from the camp to see where he was, but no trace of him. It was getting late at night, and I became worried. All of a sudden I heard, 'Eh, Bud,' and I turned and there was Navarra, stumbling toward the campsite on a broken foot. Come to find out he had left base camp and gone all the way to Lake Kop searching for our new campsite. Stumbling around, he had broken his foot. Possibly he had lost the location.

The suspicion that either Navarra had never found the ark (or wood on the mountain) or had indeed found wood but had lost the location, finally surfaced in 1970.

With Ralph E. Crawford as president and guided by a board of directors including members of the Arctic Institute of North America, SEARCH Foundation decided to launch a full-scale expedition to the mountain to drill and excavate the ice mass in which Navarra claimed he had seen the shadow of the ark. The basis for their optimism was a short probe the foundation had conducted during the summer of 1969, which had resulted in the actual location of pieces of wood identical to that of the Navarra find. It was on July 31, the ninth day of the 1969 adventure, that Navarra revealed the site.

"On that day, Navarra and I were climbing together and sat down on this rock. . . . I knew we were getting close to the area because where I was led [by Navarra] last year was one more notch up," Bud taped in Istanbul.

"Navarra put his arm around me and said, 'Bud, *ici!* This is it.' I looked at him, and he noticed I was surprised because last year he had led me to another spot!

"Then he said, 'The ark of Noah is underneath here.' Something told me not to say a word. It should have been another 300 or 500 feet up.

"We started digging—and we found wood!"

Treated initially with secrecy, the find was soon widely publicized by SEARCH Foundation as the first serious verification that Noah's ark had indeed been found. Referring to the Navarra site as the probable resting spot for Noah's ark, SEARCH president Crawford admitted to Navarra, "If yours is not the correct area, we have no other clue on the whole mountain."

Soon after the return of the expedition, Bud Crawford, Elfred Lee, and others began openly to question the reliability of Navarra's claims, and new dating reports heightened their uneasiness.

Anxious for scientific confirmation, Elfred Lee, a board member of SEARCH, had mailed out wood specimens to various institutions, requesting a carbon-14 dating. Two samples—"N" representing wood Navarra found in 1955; and "O" representing wood found by Navarra and SEARCH in 1969, were mailed to Geochron Laboratories, Inc., Cambridge, Massachusetts. The University of Pennsylvania received only one sample of wood, identified "O." On September 12, 1969, the results came in, and they were shattering.

The two samples submitted to Geochron Laboratories showed different readings when subjected to the Carbon-14 dating method. Sample "N" revealed its age as 1,690 years with a variant of plus or minus 120 years. Using 1950 as a year of reference, the wood dated to A.D. 260. Sample "O" didn't fare any better. It gave a reading of 1,350 with a variant of plus or minus 95 years, placing the death of that tree at A.D. 600.

On October 15, 1969, another report was received at foundation headquarters. This was the testing report from the physics department of the University of Pennsylvania, and it, too, submitted dates that could not have any possible connection with the ark of Noah. Processed under Lab. No. P-1620, the wood revealed A.D. 627 plus/minus 48 years and A.D. 587 plus/minus 49 years as its probable age.

Is it conceivable that this wood was of a different type than that originally found by Navarra? Was it possible that *his* reported carbon dating of 4,484 years could have been obtained from another sample? For a fleeting moment this thought crossed the minds of foundation officers, but the second sheet from the University of Pennsylvania found in the envelope decried that possibility. It was a copy of a letter written by Dr. Francis Kukachka of the Wood Identification Bureau of the United States Department of Agriculture Forest Service, addressed to Dr. Elisabeth F. Ralph of the University of Pennsylvania:

"Reference is made to your letter of September 3, and wood specimen P-1620 from Mount Ararat, Turkey.

"*The wood is identified as belonging to the white oak group* (Quercus sp.), but the exact species cannot be determined on the basis of the wood alone. The dark color and hardness of the wood is characteristic of white oak wood which has been exposed for a long period of time to water containing iron. The tannin in the wood reacts with the iron producing the characteristic color and hardness and apparently makes the wood very resistant to natural degradation.

"*A number of years ago I received wood of this same type from the same area from the Archaeological Research Foundation of New York.*"

It was in fact the same type of wood that Navarra had discovered and had submitted to ARF for possible identification some years before. SEARCH had indeed reached the Navarra site, *but whereas Navarra's wood had received a carbon-14 dating of 4,484 years by an institute whose identity was not revealed to us, the two Geochron samples yielded respectively 1,690 plus/*

minus 120 years and 1,350 plus/minus 95 years, and the University of Pennsylvania reported datings of *1,342 plus/minus 48 and 1,382 plus/minus 49 years.* To reemphasize their results, the University of Pennsylvania went one step further and submitted parts of their samples to a British carbon dating station, which "derived about the same dates during an independent analysis," according to Dr. Froelich Rainey, museum director and archaeologist of the University of Pennsylvannia. The discrepancy in results, using the same methods, was too obvious.

There was little doubt now. The 1969 SEARCH team under the guidance of Fernand Navarra had reached Navarra's site, had found "Navarra wood," had believed it might be part of the ark of Noah; but the carbon-14 dating presented an almost insurmountable obstacle.

SEARCH was far from dead however. Within weeks the reports were forgotten, for there were more important issues to be considered. Critics bombarded lecturing members of SEARCH with the same question. "The Bible story says the ark was made of gopher wood; yet your sample is white oak– Care to explain?" they'd ask. And invariably SEARCH officials would try to overcome this obstacle by attempting to persuade them that possibly the inside of the ship had been made of white oak—and the outside of gopher. The matter of claiming that the wood sample had been "impregnated with pitch" also exposed SEARCH to criticism, for a diligent examination of the files of SEARCH has never produced a chemical analysis report establishing that the wood had been impregnated with pitch. It was merely a piece of old oak. Nothing more—nothing less.

Despite such questions, plans were laid for a million-dollar expedition for 1970. It coincided with my joining SEARCH. Located in the nation's capital, it was always easy for SEARCH to publicize its news via Washington's newspaper correspondents. The foreign press also had expressed extreme interest in this new probe for the ship, and newspaper clippings from both

The late A. J. Smith, Ph.D., D.D., president of the Oriental Archaeological Research Expedition. An ardent ark-researcher, Dr. Smith was the first to lead an expedition to Mount Ararat in the postwar years.

Mount Ararat, as painted by Elfred Lee.

ELFRED LEE

The Chinese word for "ship" consists of the symbols for "mouth" and "eight." To some this suggests that the ark was a boat which carried eight persons.

Nu-Wah is regarded as an ancient Chinese ancestor and hero. The Chinese characters in this name are not used for their meaning but for their sound. Thus Nu-Wah (Noah?) could be indicated as the ancestor of the Chinese.

Colonel Alexander A. Koor of the White Russian Army submitted much material to the various ark organizations. This map shows the Ararat area together with his comments.

Archeology of Ararats and Vicinity Still Untouched by Investigation

Archeological Sites and Data on Mt.Ararat and the surrounding region.

by Col. Alexander A. Koor.

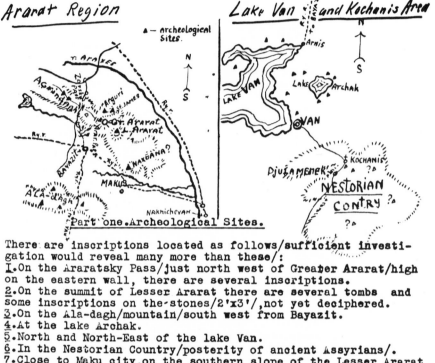

Part one.Archeological Sites.

There are inscriptions located as follows/sufficient investigation would reveal many more than these/:

1.On the Araratsky Pass/just north west of Greater Ararat/high on the eastern wall, there are several inscriptions.
2.On the summit of Lesser Ararat there are several tombs and some inscriptions on the stones/2'x3'/,not yet deciphered.
3.On the Ala-dagh/mountain/south west from Bayazit.
4.At the lake Archak.
5.North and North-East of the lake Van.
6.In the Nestorian Country/posterity of ancient Assyrians/.
7.Close to Maku city,on the southern slope of the Lesser Ararat thereare the ruins of the ancient town Naxuana,here is tomb of Patriarch Noah,according to Armenin historian Vartan.
8.On the North Eastern slope of Greater Ararat there is the ruin of the ancient site Ar-Guri.
9.Not far from Ar-Guri there is the ruin of the St. James monastary,destroyed by an earthquake in 1840/Many ancient books and relics of Noah's epoch were lost here.
10.On Agri- dagh/mountain N-E.of Greater Ararat/there is a very old road/called Colchis Road/.This area should be searched.

The inscriptions are in the following languages: Hettit,Assiro-Babilonian/Cuneiform/and Arabic-Tartar.There are some Sumerian Cuneiform inscriptions around Lake Van.

Then there are perhaps 50 or more other archeological sites in the Ararat region which have never been investigated-the ruins of ancient villages,towns,buildings,tombs,caves,etc.

Colonel Koor has gone to great lengths to supply detailed archaeological sites to the Sacred History Research Expedition. This map is part of the collection of maps and sketches now in the files of various present-day ark-exploration groups. Most of the sites marked on this map have never been explored.

Sacred History Research Expedition

"It is the glory of God to conceal a thing: but the honour of kings is to search out a matter" Prov. 25:2

FIRST MESSAGE FROM THE ARARAT REGION
By Col. Alexander A. Koor

Some inscriptions of Karada (Kara-dagh?)

I. Some inscriptions which I found and copied in the year 1915 in the region of Mt. Ararat:

1. . . . .

2. . . . .

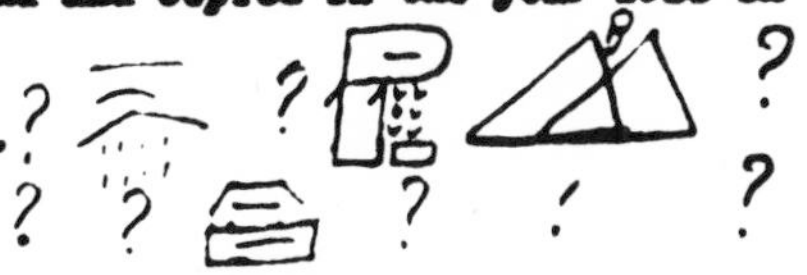

I translated the pictorial signs and they give me an accurate explanation of the origin of the words MAGOG, GOG, etc. (Ezekiel 38:2 and 39:1) This explanation also upholds the truth and accuracy of Chapter 10 end of Genesis. In short, the words Magog, Gog are words of the Sumerian tongue, which shows the ancient origin of the words. Jews incorporated the words through the Assiro-Babylonians: The word MAGOG consists of two words: MA and GOG.

The word MA is a pictorial sign of which is  and in cuneiform: 

It means: (1) "origin, (2) "the seeds of the waters (FLOOD)".

The word GOG, his pictorial sign is  and in cuneiform: 

It means: (1) "the Word of GOD" or "by the Word of GOD."
(2) "thrown" or "banished by GOD."

Having two meanings: 

Pictorial sign -"originating from (by) the Word of GOD" and "the seeds of the waters (FLOOD), thrown by GOD", are both amazingly coincidental with BIBLE text. Noah came in Mt. Ararat's region with the Flood, that is, with the waters. Likewise, the first meaning: "Originating with the Word of God", is upheld in Chapter 1, Verses 1, 2, 3, The Gospel of St. John.

The word GOG is met with in the text "Ishtar", from the library of the temple Ishtar in Nipur, and also in the text of "7 tablets of the Creation of the World", part 6, p. 11. For linguistical disbelievers of Ancient Ball "Sumerians", pictorial signs, as proof.

Pictorial sign  is read: TU KOOR and means: "to come to rest on mountains" or "peak". Cuneiform:  "KOOR" means, mountain, river. (Koora or Kura.)

Pictorial sign  is read: TOOB and means: "to filled earth." (TUB-AL)

This report by Colonel Alexander A. Koor has often been regarded as a copy and translation of the first message ever inscribed in the Ararat region. Copied in the year 1915 while he was stationed there, these inscriptions are said to be only a part of a general Flood account.

Archbishop Nouri, Nestorian priest, archdeacon of Babylon and sacred crown's supreme representative-general of the holy orthodox patriarchal imperiality. In 1893 Nouri startled industrialists in Belgium and the United States by proposing to haul Noah's ark down the mountain and have it reassembled at the Chicago World's Fair. He claimed to be the first "modern" discoverer of Noah's ark.

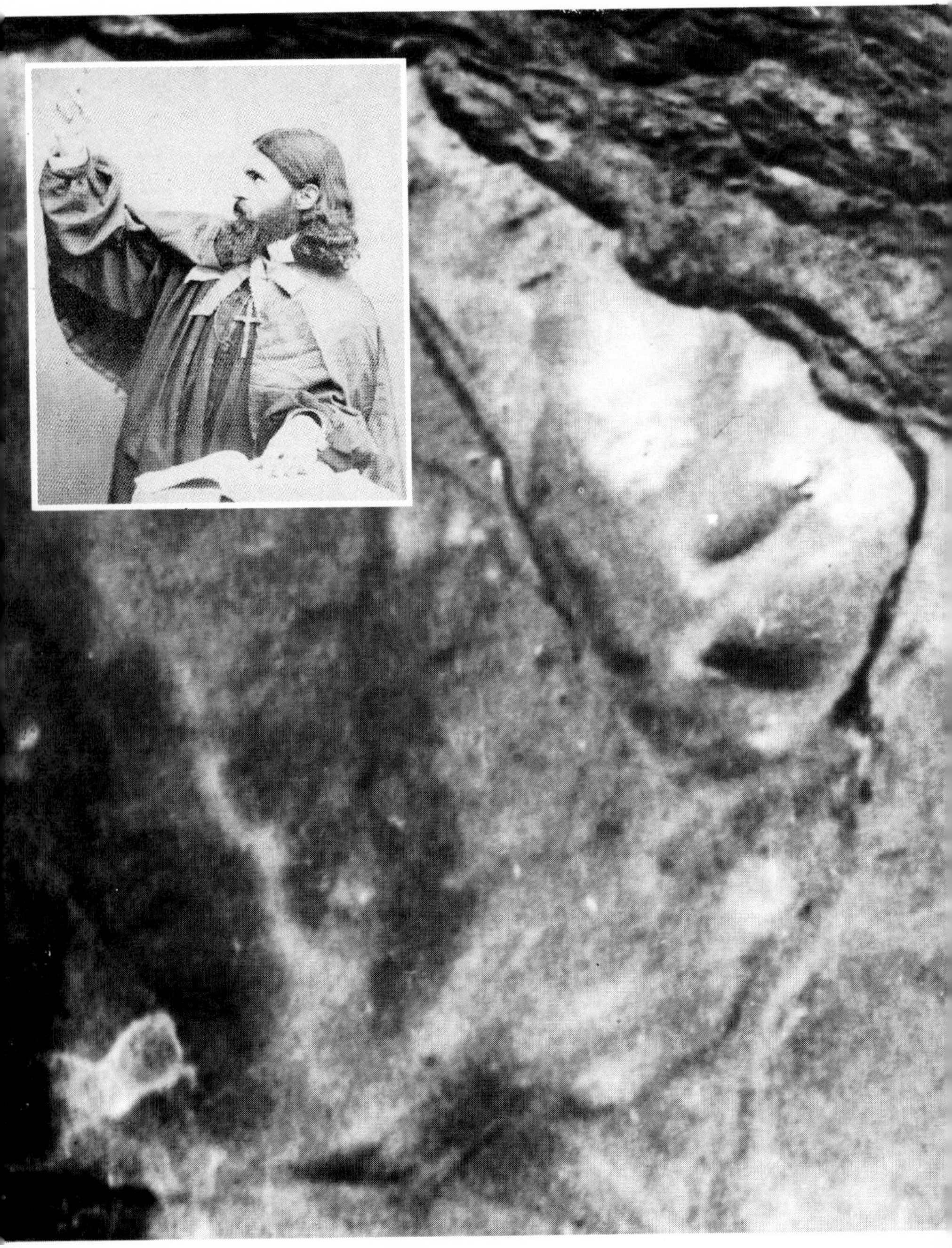

This aerial photograph caused much excitement in 1960. From an apparent lava stream in eastern Turkey a strange shiplike object protrudes. The expedition which investigated

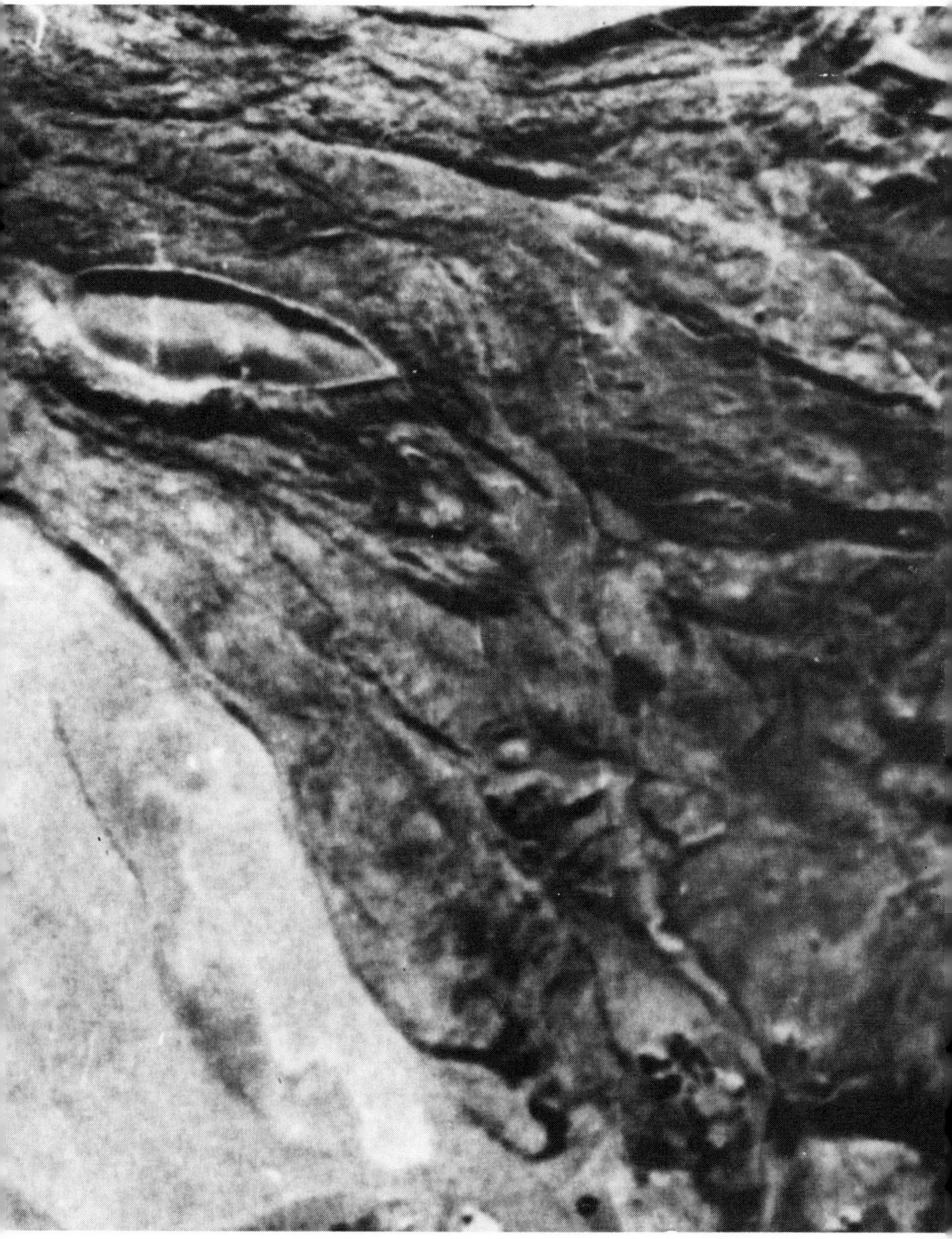

the site pulled back hurriedly without conclusive evidence as to its identity.

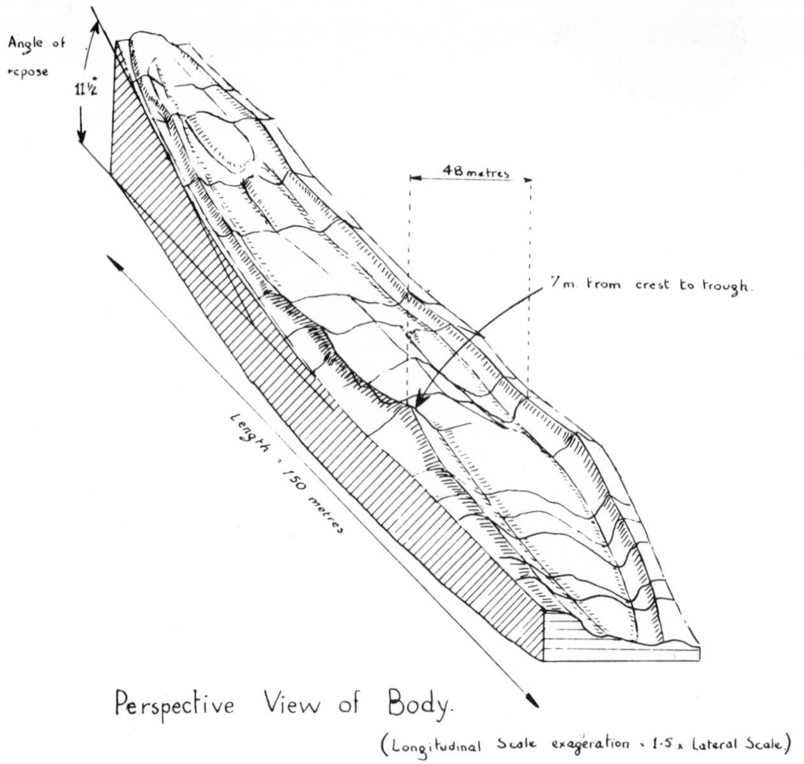

When studied with the stereoplanograph, the aerial photograph revealed some interesting aspects. Arthur Brandenburger, professor of photogrammetry at Ohio State University, maintains that all his scientific calculations backed the original conclusion that the shape was indeed a ship of approximately 450 feet in length.

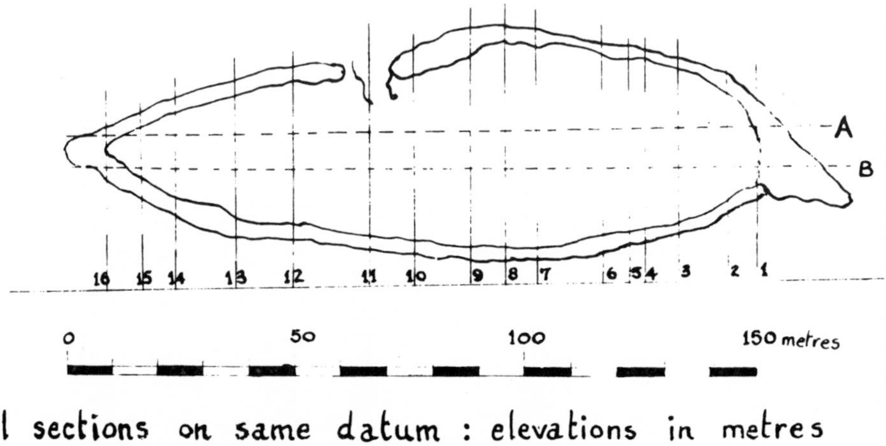

"Grand plan" of the boat-shaped object according to measurements by the stereoplanograph. Having studied the phenomenon both by photograph and in the field during the 1960 expedition, Brandenburger still felt that the shape may cover the ark. "A sole surface archaeological investigation of only two days," he said, "is not sufficient to entitle us to state that the formation is not the ark."

Rene Noorbergen stands on the boat-shaped earth formation investigated by the 1960 expedition.

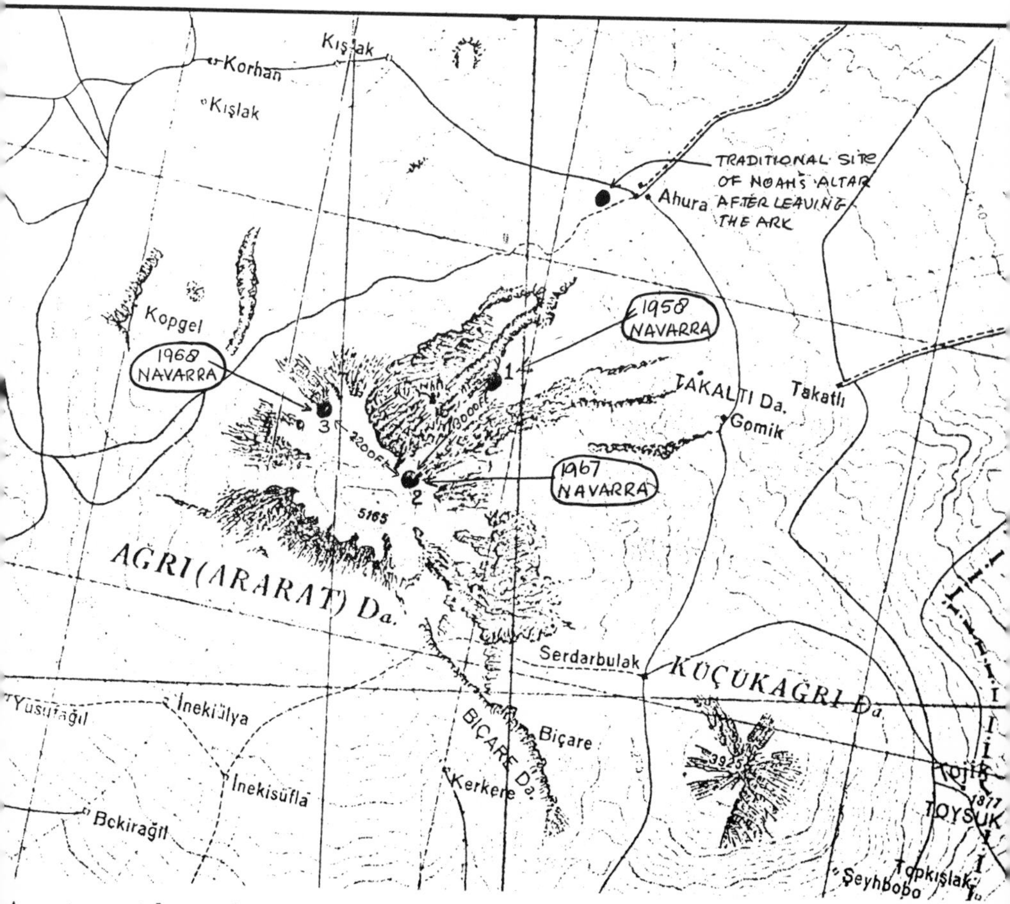

A controversial map showing the different sites reported by Fernand Navarra as the spot where Noah's ark may be located. Sites No. 1 and No. 2 are 3,000 feet apart, and No. 2 and No. 3 are 2,200 feet apart. The elevations are also different.

Ralph Lenton of the Arctic Institute of North America (left), together with Fernand Navarra on an icepack in which ancient wood was found.

Fernand Navarra, the French demolition expert, with the ark model built for him according to designs suggested by various traditions and reported sightings of the remains of the artifact.

Based on interviews the author and Elfred Lee had with George Hagopian, Lee drew this picture, which Hagopian said is an excellent likeness of what he saw as a young shepherd boy on Mount Ararat.

George Hagopian, the Armenian who related to SEARCH Foundation his story of havin
climbed on the historical ark when he was a shepherd boy. His account resembles othe
eye witness accounts, and many consider his story reliable.

A piece of the wood, showing signs of having been cut and shaped, discovered by Navarra in 1955. Navarra believes this piece was used in the construction of the ark more than 4,000 years ago.

A sketch made by Elfred Lee, member of the 1969 expedition, depicting Navarra digging for wood during his 1955 trip to Mount Ararat. This sketch is believed to give a correct concept of how the French explorer found the collection of timbers frozen in the ice.

the United Press and overseas papers revealed a growing acceptance for the project around the globe.

Perhaps it was this increased momentum overseas that caused a disenchanted reader to voice his bitterness to us, contained in an unproved accusation.

A letter written by Jeane de Riquer, the man who, according to the Bordeaux newspapers had been the leader of the "first Navarra expedition" in 1952, bluntly informed us that he, de Riquer, had caught Navarra attempting to buy ancient wood at the foot of the mountain. It caused a short flurry of excitement at the foundation office; for an accusation of this nature, combined with the carbon-14 datings, the wood identification, and the absence of a chemical report supporting the bituminous pitch claim could really be disastrous. Only three members—Elfred Lee, Hugo Neuberg, and Ralph E. Crawford—read it; then it disappeared until the day in late November, 1973, when I launched a trial balloon at the home of Fernand Navarra.

"Do you still have the Jeane de Riquer letter in which he voiced an unproved accusation of seeing you attempting to buy ancient wood at the foot of the mountain in 1952?" I queried casually. "The letter mailed to you by the foundation in March, 1970?" That was the month in which the de Requer letter was received and disappeared at the foundation.

Navarra exploded into a violent barrage of French which, when translated by Raphael, was highly uncomplimentary for de Riquer.

He then began to explain the background of the controversy existing between de Riquer and himself, which within two sentences seemed to deteriorate in a matter of claims, counterclaims, and accusations, getting more heated in the process. I let the matter rest, for my question had been answered. There was certainly no safer place for that probably unsupported accusation than in the hands of Navarra, as he would naturally never divulge the contents of this highly negative charge. With the letter returned to France, together with an enclosed assurance saying that "it doesn't affect our thinking in the least concerning you," SEARCH proceeded with its fund raising for the 1970 expedition.

There remained only one issue, and as yet this has never been resolved. Why did Navarra give different locations of his 1952 discovery to different people? His directions wandered—sometimes by several thousand feet—even to people with whom he agreed to cooperate.

Eryl Cummings, an ark researcher, has made a careful comparison of the Navarra claims and is in agreement with Bud Crawford that there are serious discrepancies in the Navarra accounts.

"During the first years of our correspondence together," Cummings related "he mailed me a copy of his French book, and in it was a picture taken in the Ahora Gorge from the westerly side to the easterly side, facing the gorge. Underneath the picture was the caption, 'This is where I found the Ark of Noah.' The picture was shot from where I place mark No. 1. (See illustration.)

"Next, at the 1967 board meeting of ARF in New York, I recall that Navarra was shown a photograph of the northerly face of the mountain, complete with ice cap and all, and was asked to place a mark on the photograph showing where he had found the ark. (This was the meeting at which he requested help for a $120,000 loan or grant, so we can assume that he was sincere.) But when he put that mark on the photograph, it apparently was at a spot we call 'point four,' which is at the westerly side of the Ahora Gorge, right at the ice line. This is mark No. 2.

"Then in 1968, when Mr. Navarra went to Ararat with Bill Dougal and Bud Crawford, I understand from Crawford that he showed Dougal a spot next to Ark Rock on the easterly side of the Parrot Glacier as the location, while the following day he pointed out to him still another location as the correct one. This is mark No. 3."

All SEARCHers were aware of these discrepancies, but they were judged to be unimportant, and the planning of the 1970 expedition continued.

With high-ranking Mormons in the organization, Pentecostalist Demos Shakarian as adviser, and oilmen Jack Grim and Bunker Hunt as financiers, the road to the ark seemed smooth and unobstructed. An interesting point developed in early February, 1970. By chance I was standing in the office of Jeane Dixon when she received an urgent call from H. L. Hunt, the Texas billionaire. Hunt, it seemed, had been asked by SEARCH to donate funds to the ark expedition. Having faith in the psychic ability of his friend Jeane Dixon, he phoned to ask for her advice.

"I'll have to meditate on it, H. L.," I remember Jeane telling him kindly. "I'll let you know by March thirty-first. Give me a call around that time."

Replacing the phone, she turned to me.

"Rene, you're involved in this thing." She smiled, scanning my face for a reaction. "H. L. wants to know if the ark is really on the mountain. Tell me, is it *really* there?" Not knowing the answer, and not wanting to be her spiritual inspiration, I merely shrugged my shoulders. SEARCH never collected a major donation from H. L. Hunt.

Soon the Korean Freedom and Cultural Foundation's Colonel Pak, a friend of one of the board members, developed the outline for a one-million-piece mailing program. Within weeks, 600,000 pieces of promotion were dropped in the mailboxes of conservative Republicans, and the money began pouring in. During that time a curious phone call was received at the headquarters of SEARCH, and the resulting conversation eventually brought me into personal contact with a man who may have been one of the last Armenians ever to see the holy ark.

One of the letters dropped into the mailbox of Mrs. Mary Board, a semiretired real estate broker, and it was responsible for the contact. It filled her with a nervous excitement when she read it.

Within minutes she picked up the phone.

Elfred Lee answered.

"There's this old friend of mine in Easton, Maryland," she explained hurriedly to Lee, a SEARCH board member. "An old Armenian, George Hagopian, says he saw the ark when he was still a little boy. Reading your letter brings it all back to me. I've known him for many years, and he has told my husband and me the story of his visit to the ark many times since our first meeting. He says he used to live right at the foot of the mountain.

"Would you people be interested in talking to him?"

Would we ever!

One of the most difficult tasks in this line of research is tracking down competent and reliable witnesses, and to find one living so close by was almost beyond expectations. In a few days Elfred Lee arranged the first personal contact with Mary Board and George Hagopian, and a week later he returned for another interview. Both sessions yielded promising information, and after listening to the tape recordings, Eryl Cummings and I set up an appointment with him to fill in some of the holes in the story.

Spooning up lukewarm soup in a smelly diner in Easton, Maryland, we sat fascinated, listening to George Hagopian recall his early days as a poor shepherd boy who guided his restless flocks on the grassy slopes of Mount Ararat.

"In those days," George mused, his words heavy with an unmistakable Armenian accent, "my uncle and I used to climb the slope of the mountain to herd the sheep. Everyone who was able used to take their sheep to the green zone of the mountain and graze them there. At daytime there was no problem at all. Just the very idea of accompanying the older men to the slopes of the holy mountain fascinated us—but those nights!"

He closed his eyes for a moment, reliving his boyhood impressions.

"Then the wolves would come and the bear, and we'd burn the campfires high to keep our sheep safe. The dogs would run and bark all night, checking the flocks and scaring the wolves that would come down the mountain to catch just one little lamb."

George paused, and I quickly threw in a question, hoping that he'd now talk about the artifact.

"Were you with your uncle when you first saw the ark?" I asked.

"Yes, I first went there when I was about ten years old. It must have been around 1902. My grandfather was the minister of the big Armenian Orthodox Church in Van, and he always told me stories about the holy ship on the holy mountain.

"And then one day my uncle said, 'Georgie, I'm going to take you to the holy mountain,' and he took me with him, packed his supplies on his donkey, and together we started our trek toward Mount Ararat.

" 'Uncle, that's the holy mountain,' I said, pointing to what seemed to be our destination up ahead of us.

" 'That's right, Georgie,' he said. 'Massis is the holy mountain.'

"My feet were getting sore, and the donkey kept wanting to go in the wrong direction, but we continued climbing until we got about halfway. Then Uncle took both supplies and me on his back, and we climbed and climbed.

"It took us almost eight days from the time we left Van to the moment we got to the place on the holy mountain where both my grandfather and my uncle had said the holy ship had come to rest.

"I guess my uncle took me there that year because it was a year without much snow," Hagopian said. "A 'smooth year,' we called it. There's one of those about every twenty years.

"And then we got to the ark—" George stopped, groping for the exact words to describe his recollections as clearly as he could.

"I said, 'Uncle, it's so dark around here. Nothing but mist. Is this the top of the world? Did the ark rest all the way up here?'

" 'Yes,' he said, 'this is the holy ark. This big ship right in front of you. Let me help you get on it!'

"An immense stone mass loomed threateningly ahead of me. It was like a wall, like a building. It couldn't be; it didn't look like a ship.

" 'Is this *really* the ship, Uncle?' I asked, touching the towering object. 'This is stone, not wood!'

" 'It's the ship all right, Georgie,' he answered. 'Come, help me. I'll prove it to you.'

"He dropped his pack to the ground, and together he and I began to haul stones and huge boulders to the side of the ship. Uncle was a big man, well over six feet tall and very powerful, and within a short time he had stacked a pile of rocks against the side of the ship. Higher and higher we piled them until he at last told me to stop.

" 'Georgie, come here,' he said, grabbing me playfully by the arm. 'You are going on top of the holy ark.' He lifted me up and put me on his shoulders, and together we climbed the pile of rocks. When he had reached the top, his hands grabbed my ankles and he began to push me up.

" 'Reach for the top, Georgie,' he yelled. 'Grab the edge and pull yourself up!'

A tear welled up in the old Armenian's eyes. He was reliving those nostalgic moments all over again and didn't care whether his emotions were showing. It was *his* youth he was recalling, and without us as a soundingboard it would have been only a voiceless memory.

But now it had life, and he continued: "I stood up straight and looked all over the ship. It was long, all right. I realize that things always seem larger to a child, but looking back now, I am sure it must have been at least 1,000 feet long and more than 600 feet wide. The height was about forty feet or more.

" 'Look inside the ark,' my uncle called up to me. 'Look for the holes. Look for the big one. Look inside and tell me what you see.'

"I shivered from the cold and from fear and glanced around me. Yes, there was the hole, big and gaping. Was that the one he meant? It looked so mysterious.

" 'Uncle, I'm scared,' I yelled down to him. 'I see a large black hole in the top. Don't make me go in there, please!'

" 'Don't be scared, Georgie,' he soothed. 'There's no one in the ark. It's been empty for a long time. Don't worry about it.'

"I peeked into the blackness of the hole, but saw nothing. Then I knelt down and kissed the holy ark."

"Did you see anything else while you were up there?" I interrupted him. "Any other distinguishing marks that we might use for identification if and when we locate the object?"

George Hagopian nodded his head affirmatively. His eyes glistened with excitement.

"Oh, yes, many things. There's the moss—that green growth that covers the entire ark. Also when we were there, the top of the ark was covered with a very thin coat of fresh fallen snow, but when I brushed some of it away I could see the green moss growing right on top. When I pulled a piece off, it looked as if the rock was made of wood. The grain was right there. This green moss, it made the ark feel soft and moldy. My uncle took his gun and shot into the side of the ark but the bullet wouldn't penetrate. It just dropped when it hit the side. The whole ark was petrified, turned to rock."

"Did you see anything on the roof besides one large hole?"

"Yes, I remember *small* holes running all the way from the front to the back," Hagopian answered. "I don't know exactly how many, but there must have been at least fifty of them running down the middle with small intervals in between.

"After describing the holes to my uncle, I asked, 'What are these for, Uncle?'

" 'They're holes for air, Georgie,' he said. 'A long time ago there used to be animals and people in the ark, and that's why they had those holes in there. There's one special hole too where Noah let the dove fly out.'

" 'Where did they all go, Uncle?' I asked.

" 'They just left, Georgie,' he said. 'They're gone. The holy ship is completely empty now.'

"Uncle pulled his long hunting knife from his belt, and with the heavy handle he chipped a piece from the side of the ark.

" 'Uncle, I want to get off,' I yelled down to him. 'I'm scared. Will you catch me?'

" 'Sure,' he said, 'but don't jump too wildly.' So I let myself down the side of the ship until I felt his hands take my ankles in a firm grip. Gently he let me down, and together we went back down the mountainside.

"The first thing I did when I arrived in Van was to see my grandfather.

" 'Grandfather, I've been to the holy ark,' I said proudly, filled with enthusiasm. 'Uncle took me up there. I've been *on* it. I've looked into the hole!'

"Overcome by the news, Grandfather hugged me, misty-eyed.

" 'Georgie, someday you will become a holy man,' he whispered, trying to keep his voice from breaking. 'You will be a holy man because you've been on God's holy ark.'

"He never found out whether his dream for me ever came true, for a few years later he died at Van."

Intriguing as the story was, the details of the sighting were a bit too hazy, and for another three hours, Eryl Cummings and I grilled Hagopian in a friendly way, extracting more facts, especially those that could be useful in our search for the ship's exact location.

By sifting and comparing his various statements, we were able to zero in on precise questions, and George was more than willing to supply the answers from his slowly fading memory.

"I saw the ark a second time," he recalled. "I think it was in 1904. We were on the mountain looking for holy flowers, and I went back to the ark and it looked still the same. Nothing had changed. I didn't get to the top that time, but stayed at the side, and really got a good look at it. It was resting on a steep ledge of bluish-green rock about 3,000 feet wide. Another thing I noticed was that I didn't see any nails at all. It seemed that the whole ship was made of one piece of petrified wood. I could even see the grain of the wood even though the ship had already turned to stone."

"How about windows and doors?" I asked.

"Oh, no! There were no windows in the ship, of that I am certain," he answered emphatically, his mind's eye roaming the sides of the ship. "And there was definitely no door in the side of the ship that I could see. No opening of any kind. There may have been one in the part I couldn't see, but that I don't know. That side was practically inaccessible. I could only see my side and part of the bow."

"What was the shape of the ship? Was it perfectly straight? Was it rectangular, or what?"

Hagopian paused for a moment before answering, for the waitress had come by to pick up our soup bowls. George waited until she was gone.

"That roof was flat with the exception of that narrow raised section running all the way from the bow to the stern with all those holes in it. The sides were slanting outward to the top," he continued, "and the front was flat, too. You know, I didn't see any real curves. It was unlike any other boat I have ever seen. It looked more like a flat-bottomed barge."

"But the location, George. Can you describe the location of the ship on the mountain? Are there any specific landmarks?"

The answer came slowly but unhesitantly.

"I do remember that one side of the mountain is impossible to climb," he explained. "My uncle and I went through Bayazit, close to the border, and climbed the mountain from the direction of Azerbaidzhan. I recall trees and orchards, somewhere between ten and fifteen thousand feet on the mountain. We used to eat the fruit whenever we could. I am sure that if the scenery hasn't changed too much, I could take you right to the spot; but at my age, climbing Massis may not be that easy."

Hagopian's statement that the ship he had seen had already been petrified brought us to the subject of the wood discovered by Navarra in 1955 and by SEARCH in 1969. Asking his opinion as to its possible origin, he replied patiently: "Listen, son, I don't believe that wood is part of Noah's ark. The ark I saw was made of wood, *petrified wood,* not wood that can be cut. Also you said the wood was found at an elevation of approximately 14,000 feet. This proves that it cannot be the ark, for what I saw was much higher.

"But don't take my word for it. Wait until you have located the real ark, and then you'll see that there is no connection at all.

"Perhaps the wood you've found is part of an early construction on the mountain; maybe it's a section of a house or a temple. I don't know. But I do know the real ark is petrified, and I do know it's on the mountain."

His tired voice trailed off. He was weary, and it showed. A recent eighteen-day bout in the hospital for treatment of the after-effects of an injury he had sustained more than fifty years ago while in the Turkish army had taken a heavier toll than he had at first admitted.

I pulled another map from my attaché case and compared his recollection of the possible location of the artifact with my knowledge acquired over the years of research, and immediately there was a generation gap. Whereas I was speaking of the mountain being in Turkey, he had the impression it was still in Russia, even though barely across the Turkish border.

Another point which complicated his endeavor to locate his spot on the map was that our map was too general in nature and covered too large an area. Having never seen a map as a child, it was nigh impossible for him to match his childhood memory against the printed reference points.

Five long hours after first meeting George Hagopian, I dropped him off at his home.

He grabbed my hand in a viselike grip; too strong a handshake for a man his age.

"Come back, please," he pleaded, his eyes still sparkling. "You're always welcome. Perhaps I'll go back someday, but only if I can be sure I can make the trip.

"But *you* go. You find the ark. I know it's there. I was there seventy years ago, and I saw it!"

George turned, and, kicking the autumn leaves with his shuffling feet, he began walking toward his simple wooden-framed house.

His desire to return once again to his homeland was never realized, for he died less than a year after our interview. Obviously, the aging memories of Hagopian cannot be reconciled with the reported discoveries of Navarra.

When the initial Hagopian contact was first being examined by SEARCH in mid-June, 1970, three of us SEARCH members, Ralph Lenton, Bud Crawford, and I were getting strangled in Turkish red tape in an attempt to secure the permit allowing the expedition to proceed to Mount Ararat. Without any publicity, Ralph Lenton, the Arctic explorer, lent to the foundation by the Arctic Institute of North America, had rushed ahead of the main body of the group to begin the difficult negotiation process. It would present problems—this everyone knew. Since World War II more than forty known expeditions had combed the mountain peaks looking for the elusive ark, and the hundreds of Ararat permit requests the Turks processed every year made the selection task extremely time-consuming for them.

Fully confident that SEARCH would receive official permission to penetrate the Turkish-Russian fortification zone, an advance party of two SEARCH members had climbed the mountain and set up a small base camp on the slopes of Ararat, endeavoring to carry out some preliminary work. But due to a friendship between one of our co-workers and a prominent newsman, our carefully devised plans caved in.

"Don't talk about it to anyone," he mysteriously confided to the bureau chief of Associated Press in Ankara, "but we're back in town waiting for another permit. In the meantime, however, we already have two men on the mountain, without permission, of course."

The reaction was immediate. Having a well-developed news sense, the bureau chief dashed to the nearest teletype and spread the word. The news sparked excitement throughout Turkey, and the army quickly dispatched a squad to the slopes of the mountain to erase this illegal entry of SEARCH.

What this did to the expedition's chance for survival is easily predictable. Traveling feverishly between Istanbul and Ankara, Ralph Lenton and I desperately sought to placate the hurt feelings of the Turkish officials who felt betrayed, while at the same time we still pressed for permission. The final target date for the start of the expedition rapidly approached, but Turkish approval was nowhere in sight. Even political contacts that had proved to be helpful in past years seemed powerless in the wake of anti-expedition propaganda that appeared in every influential newspaper. The press criticism swelled to a crescendo of accusations and innuendos, and suddenly I was taken back to 1949 when the Russians accused the Smith expedition of espionage.

Some of the journalists had indeed done their homework well. They had patched bits and pieces together and concluded that all the search parties were in reality nothing but clumsily disguised spy operations. They had many arguments in their favor. Their reasoning was simple but understandable.

"Look," they wrote, "if all these people definitely know that the ark is there, why haven't they found it yet? They've been coming here since 1945, and it is always the same excuse. But really, can it be because Ararat borders on Russia? Or can it perhaps be a case of one ally spying on another?"

Perhaps it was this public espionage accusation that solidified the government's opposition against SEARCH. As one Turkish journalist commented to me: "What else do you expect? We know that your chairman of the board is a former FBI man, and we know that one of your leaders claims to be working for the CIA. In former years some other expeditions have come from the U.S. with U.S. Army equipment and full military support. Can you blame us for being skeptical?"

Believing that it was due to a lack of adequate representation on our part, financier Jack Grim joined us for a final effort.

Armed with a bulging file folder of security reports on members of SEARCH, he entered the office, and within seconds our fate was announced.

"Permission is refused for reasons of national security!"

Did the officer know more about the affiliations of certain members than I did?

I am sure I will never find out, but the overtones were there.

Gone was a dream. Gone was the money contributed to the project by several thousand sincere Christians.

"And by the way," the security chief added almost as an afterthought while leaving the office, "when you leave here go west. Not east. Just a suggestion, mind you!" But it was a forceful one, and home we went.

For SEARCH it meant an untimely death.

REFERENCES

1. Violet M. Cummings, *Noah's Ark, Fact or Fable?* page 182.
2. *Ibid.*, pp. 182, 183.
3. Fernand Navarra in *Atlas Magazine,* February, 1965.

CHAPTER 7

The timeless story of trying to discover Noah's ark has always been an experience of interlocking reports—a seemingly continuous loop without end. Judging from the ever-increasing number of eyewitnesses who have in recent years added their versions to the already bursting files, many more variations of the same basic tale will be born before the final discovery is made.

The seventies were no different in this respect.

After the unfortunate events that blocked the 1970 expedition, SEARCH Foundation retreated from Ankara with only the faintest hope for its doubtful future. But even though the foundation failed in its attempts, efforts to find the ship were far from finished.

While the 1970 fiasco was still fresh in the minds of the concerned parties and we were still pondering the implications of the George Hagopian account, an even more spectacular bit of information came hedging around the corner, waiting to be captured.

It was Violet Cummings who accidentally started it all.

Just having completed the manuscript for her book *Noah's Ark: Fact or Fable?* she was anxious to see it promoted in the local bookstore. The young man who picked up the phone in the store wasn't at all surprised about the request.

It was the title that startled him.

"Noah's ark—a book about finding the ark?" he queried. "Oh, I know something about that. That ship was found years ago when I was still at the Smithsonian." Having never heard anything about a discovery by the Smithsonian Institution, she exclaimed, "I have not heard about this. How come you didn't tell anyone else about it—or did you?"

"No, I didn't, because no one ever asked me," Daryl Davis* answered. "You'd be surprised at all the things they have behind locked doors!"

By now her initial reaction had changed to nervous excitement. Could this possibly be the one lead all "ark-eologists" were waiting for? Was it possible that an official body like the Smithsonian Institution had finally discovered the ship and had not revealed it to the world?

The coincidence of meeting in her hometown on the Navajo reservation a twenty-one-year-old boy who possessed just the right information didn't seem extraordinary to her. Ark people are used to happenings like that.

But the Smithsonian Institution?

For many years expeditions have repeatedly attempted to interest the Smithsonian and the National Geographic Society in the project, but both professional organizations have always shied away from any form of cooperation with the amateur archaeologists. In fact, the Smithsonian disclaimed any belief in the ark's survival. The National Geographic was slightly more flexible, but only to the extent of supplying film to one of the expeditions with the condition that they would have first rights to the photographs of a possible discovery. But that was all. They had little faith in the existence of any such artifact as Noah's ark on Ararat or anywhere else.

The missing link in the controversy is the ark. If it could be

---

*Real name withheld to avoid embarrassment.

found on a height of say 14,000 feet, then a universal Deluge becomes credible. It is unrealistic to believe that in the dawn of history an immense army of relatively uneducated tribesmen would literally carry hundreds of tons of heavy timber up the treacherous slopes of Mount Ararat and build a ship at the 14,000-foot level and leave it there—just to confuse us gullible beings of the twentieth century.

Finding the ark might indeed seriously undermine certain theories of both modern archaeology and geology, and it is rather difficult to imagine that dedicated evolutionists would go out of their way to search for an object that would tear at their fundamental doctrines.

Within days after the first contact, an exuberant Eryl Cummings phoned me from Washington's National Airport. He'd given me some scant details about the Davis development and had come to track down the facts of the case. Later, while we sat in the quiet of my library in my Virginia home, he shared his tape-recorded interview of the young bookseller with me. It most assuredly surpassed all other accounts I had ever encountered.

With a cold, metallic quality, the recorded voices resounded throughout the room.

"Mr. Davis, we learned about you from my wife's call to the bookstore," he explained, "and in talking with you she learned that you had at some time in the past been working with the Smithsonian, and the interesting story you told her. I wish you would recall your experience and [tell us] of your knowledge about the ark of Noah and the expedition to the Ararat area."

There was a pregnant pause as the tape rolled on. Then Davis's voice was heard.

"Well, about 1968, toward the end of October," he recalled, "I contacted the Smithsonian volunteer work program and offered my time for volunteer work. About the first of November I was placed in vertebrate paleontology under the direction of Dr. Robert Geist.

"Sometime in December we received from an expedition I had been told was comprised of members of the Smithsonian group and the National Geographic Society—a joint expedition —some shipments from the Mount of Ararat. Included in this were some fragments of wood believed to be from Noah's ark and a long oblong case just like a coffin containing some human remains. The pieces of wood were dark, blackened, and had bored holes in them that appeared to have been burnt out and wooden plugs extending about eight inches through.

"Also comprised in this were several photographs taken, I was told, from a balloon suspended over the site, using an infrared camera. When the photographs were interlocked," he continued, "it showed an oblong keel, a boat-shaped hull, underneath the ice. As to the size, I have no idea what to compare it with. It was comprised chiefly of a curved upsweep stern, and two oblongs which were pointed out to be steering oars or columns and a long deckhouse, quite flat. It was not two-story, it was only one. I saw no evidence of any kind of door or outside structure on the hall itself. The bow of the ark, or whatever it was, was extremely fragmented. I could only see indistinct lines underneath the ice. I had been told that portions were sticking out from the surface. Also that the expedition used thermite bombs, I believe, and melted portions of it; actually getting inside in a portion of the main superstructure where it had been broken off, I think, by a landslide.

"The coffin that was brought back was supposed to have contained a human body and was found near the hull or the second deck of the vessel. It was then taken to physical anthropology where a close friend of mine by the name of Gene Lester Rice was working like I was—volunteer labor. He opened the coffin and started the preliminary cleaning of it with acetone, when the director jumped on him and really let him know that it was none of his business who was in there. I made some inquiries to Dr. Geist concerning the body, and he told me that it was nothing to concern me and that if the religious fanatics ever found out who was in that box it would only cause trouble.

"So to keep my job I kept quiet about it, and that's really about all I know."

"Can you describe the size of the timbers or more of the shape of the portion that you did see of the ship?" Eryl asked.

"Well, it was shaped like an old-fashioned keelboat," Daryl remembered. "The stern of it was high upsweep; extremely curved on the bottom. It was big, but I have no way of knowing how big. The infrared photographs I saw [showed] the whole thing covered up except for a few fragmented timbers out to the side and the hole they bored down.

"It is a ship. It's not a building."

I shut the recorder off and looked at Cummings.

"Have you checked on Rice yet? Does he still live at Fort Belvoir?"

Cummings had not checked, so we set out to track the whereabouts of Gene Lester Rice—first through the phone directory, next the Army Public Information office. After that we checked tax record files, real estate deeds, finally ending with the Pentagon tapping their vast reservoir of computerized material stored in the Army Record Center in Saint Louis. Ironically, when we did locate the address, it was only blocks away from where we had first begun our search.

Did he know Daryl Davis? Did he remember the ark episode at the Smithsonian?

Pacing nervously up and down the family room of his home, Gene denied at the outset any knowledge of Daryl's story.

"I didn't work at the Smithsonian at all," he insisted. "He must have confused me with somebody else. He did know a lot of people in this area, but I wasn't involved."

Wasn't he?

A call placed to Davis later that day added suspicions to our initial disbelief. Daryl was emphatic in stating that it had indeed been Rice who had worked with him at the Smithsonian. What's more, he claimed they used to travel back and forth to work every day. He simply couldn't be mistaken!

This torpedoed the idea of a wrong identity. More puzzling, however, was Daryl's statement to Cummings after his return home that Rice had phoned him the moment Cummings and I had left the house and demanded to know why Daryl had blown his (Rice's) cover.

Coinciding with our visit to Rice, another bit of supporting evidence surfaced. A young Washington attorney (name withheld upon request) told us of talking with a man at a legal meeting, who mentioned to him that he had been involved in an expedition to Mount Ararat in 1968, at which time they had, among other activities, shot infrared photographs of an object they believed to be Noah's ark.

"Can't talk about it any further, though," the spokesman apologized. "I've already said too much."

A careful check by the lawyer revealed that the man was with the CIA!

The circle of mystery had widened. Whereas at first it appeared to be merely an expedition of the Smithsonian, later joined by the National Geographic, *now* the Central Intelligence Agency also seemed to have been involved. Could it be that because of this supersensitive Government involvement a lid of secrecy had been clamped down on the entire project? Could this be the reason for Rice's silence? Perhaps his father's former connection with Army Intelligence had something to do with it. With official U.S. involvement, an American expedition could certainly have penetrated Mount Ararat, using Air Force transportation and U.S. Intelligence cover. Very few Turks, with the exception of the highest ranking military, would ever have known about it, inasmuch as all activities of the group would have been conducted from U.S. air bases in eastern Turkey.

Could this really be the beginning of the end of the search for Noah's ark?

Shortly after the first interview another one followed; and, as anticipated, it added many other details to the already fascinating story. Having had time to comb his memory, Daryl now revealed that "for about three consecutive days, they brought in a lot of crates and pieces of wood and plaster casts from an expedition" from Turkey. Further, he said, when Dr. Geist had shown him the aerial photographs, he noticed that "when put together, the seven frames—the seven photographs—comprised an area, and inside it was a dark mass under the ice. He also pointed out a few wooden or stone huts on the slope."

Did Davis remember a door or entryway into the ship?

The tape of that second interview faithfully recorded his reply:

"There was no door that I saw." What he did see, however, were some primitive instruments recovered from the site.

"When these arrived at the museum," he recalled, "they were in like big blocks of earth; you know, covered with plaster, the top and bottom wrapped up. They took a vibration saw and cut the tops off all of them; cut them right in half, and these instruments were bedded down in the earth, and I was told they came right from down in here." He pointed to a sketch he had hurriedly drawn, depicting the ship as it appeared on the seven infrared frames. "This is where they found the enclosure and a couple of rough wooden buildings."

The subject of the sarcophagus, too, received attention. "Actually it was found near the bottom of the hull," he explained, "down toward the center here, all the way down. The chest itself was made of alabaster. It was a good seven feet long. One of the ends was slotted, and there's a panel that dropped down into it, with two holes on the top of the panel for a rope to haul it up." Disregarding Gene Rice's denial of any involvement,

Davis again emphasized that it had been Rice who had gone "ahead and opened the chest, and inside was either a body or a mummy. He wasn't very explicit whether it was a wrapped mummy or just a preserved body," he continued.

It was in this interview that he named Dr. Geist as the man who identified the photographs as being of the ark.

"When Geist showed me the photographs, I asked him what it was," Daryl recalled, "and he said, 'That's Noah's ark.' He said it had been driven ashore on top of this mountain, and the bow had been destroyed when it rammed into the cliff face and later the ground settled around it and broke the back of it. That's why it is in such a fragmented condition."

A harried week of checking followed, but even though available evidence definitely placed Davis in Smithsonian employ in 1968, his discovery account remained no more than a story; proof of this tremendous scientific find could nowhere be found.

Spring arrived and with it a 17,000-mile promotional tour for one of my latest books, taking me away from the research. So it remained for others to investigate the possible leads. The months rolled by, and occasional meetings with Davis added further specifics to his story. There were definite markers suggesting that he might be correct. Most promising were the details he submitted about the sarcophagus which tended to confirm the early historical reports of Noah praying daily before the body of Adam while on the high seas. One thing was certain; the ship described by Davis was not a replica of the ark as rumored to have been constructed by the Armenians as either a shrine or a burial place; for that my 1970 Jerusalem research had borne out. Could it be that this discovery was so potentially dangerous that the only thing scientists could do with it was hide it? Could it really be the controversial ark?

Almost two years passed before I inquired once again as to the status of the Davis account; but, in the interim, fragments of the story had spread to members of other interested organizations. Everywhere curious researchers collected the meager reports and patched them together, endeavoring to recreate the entire story.

In California Phyllis Watson, a school teacher's wife, commenced the painstaking task of examining every publication put out by both the National Geographic and the Smithsonian since the early 60's. She cataloged each item which would be considered a lead. Personnel lists were carefully compared; transfers of department heads recorded. Whenever a possible clue was uncovered, a similar event was looked for in the Smithsonian material and vice versa. When she first began her research, little was known that could support Davis; but with the passage of time, interesting data emerged, indicating Smithsonian/Geographic activity in eastern Turkey. Not that this could be definitely connected with Ararat, but who knows? Perhaps its real value would present itself soon. She continued her investigation. At another west coast location a medical doctor took up the challenge posed by the almost impenetrable wall of official silence. His findings opened up other avenues of research. Demanding absolute secrecy and a childlike obedience to his whims as the price for his cooperation, he attempted to shove aside other more seasoned researchers, causing some friction. With broad grins and a shrug of the shoulders, they played along, because, after all, he *did* have money, and this always helps in this type of endeavor.

The first seemingly significant clue came in November, 1973. when various rumors had Dr. Robert Geist living in either Istanbul, Izmir, or Ankara, Turkey. A quick KLM flight to the Middle East soon disproved this. I made a personal check of all the old-timers in the news business as well as in the scientific community, but my search yielded no confirmation.

Necati Dolunay, curator of the Topkapi Museum in Istanbul, also was unable to supply any leads, but he did add a positive note of another sort: "There is absolutely no possibility that a combined expedition of those two institutions could have conducted a search of Agri [Ararat] without Turkish government cooperation," he asserted. "No matter whom they worked through, the mountain is in the military zone, and to penetrate this area they would still need approval of my government. To my knowledge, no such permission has ever been granted to either a Smithsonian or a National Geographic expedition." He was an old friend (a member of the 1949 Smith expedition), and I could rely on his judgment, more so because he was usually consulted before permits of this type were granted.

Discussions with other archaeologists also did not bring Geist any closer. He seemed to have vanished after his short three-week visit to the Smithsonian.

Returning to the United States, I made a series of calls to various Smithsonian and Geographic department heads, but again the results were negative.

"No, Dr. Robert Geist never worked here," was the usual answer. "There has never been a person of that name associated with any of our projects."

Could it perhaps be a hoax? An April Fool's joke in February? The Smithsonian hierarchy undoubtedly must have realized the risk they would expose themselves to if they had actually discovered and then hidden the greatest artifact of all time.

There was only one way to find out.

Three weeks later I sat opposite Daryl Davis with the intent to extract data that would clarify his previous claims. We covered much of the same ground touched on in former interviews; yet this time the emphasis was different, for except on one point his memory had remarkably improved. Events scarcely remembered in February, 1972, now had gained new stature as additional tidbits added more luster to the thus far unsupported discovery.

In transcript form, these are the highlights of that interview:

(N) What happened was in 1968, right?

(D) Well, this is the part I am not sure about. Dates and years are hard to remember. Seems it was in '68. It was after Kennedy got killed. I guess '67, '68. That's as close as I can get.
(N) Daryl, how long did you work there?
(D) About two or three months.
(N) What part of the year?
(D) The latter part of 1968. In the fall.
(N) About Dr. Geist: Could it have been another name that sounded like it? Have you ever seen his name printed on papers or anything? Possibly Robert A. Geist?
(D) No, just Robert Geist. I don't remember a middle initial.
(N) Can you give me a description of the man?
(D) Well, he was pretty old. He wasn't young. About an inch shorter than I was. I am 5 feet 9 inches. There again, at that time I was shorter. He wasn't fat. He was stocky. Big. Just middle age. Bald on top. Had a beard—short beard. No moustache. And reddish brown hair.
(N) How about the color of his face?
(D) Red face.
(N) Did he wear glasses?
(D) He carried them. I never saw him use them though. Maybe nearsighted.
(N) About his language: Did he have an accent?
(D) Yes, he had an accent. A German accent. Noticeable. He was German.
(N) Did he ever say anything about his background? What he had done? Where he had lived?
(D) At that time I was pretty interested in World War II—history in general—and I was in the habit of stopping at a military shop on the way to work—relics and replicas—in Alexandria, and one day I got a dagger there. He was looking at it, and he told me he had been in Germany during the war. I asked whether he had been a soldier, and he said No. He had fortunately been studying. He said he went to a university outside of Bremen.

(N) There is no university outside of Bremen. Bremen didn't have a university until about four years ago.
(D) Well, he told me he studied outside of Bremen, because he was happy they were there and not in the city because they could see it being bombed. He was never in the German army.
(N) Daryl, you have sketched this thing here (pointing toward the drawing depicting the photographs of the ark). When did you sketch this? It says February, 1972. This must have been three years after you saw the originals. Did you sketch them from memory in February, 1972, based on what you saw years ago, or did you go home from the Smithsonian and sketch something like this right then?
(D) No. I sketched them really from memory, honestly. I'd say it's accurate shipwise, and the basic terrain configurations. Some of the stuff here I just put in. The alignment of the separate photographs—I just remember how it was.
(N) Is it pretty accurate?
(D) Yes, I'd say it is. I am sure if you saw the pictures and then this you'd say, "Hey, that's it!"
(N) What kind of pictures were they? Just negatives, photgraphs?
(D) I was told they were infrared photographs. The borders were trimmed off.
(N) In the size of about eight by ten?
(D) No. They were regular size. More the Polaroid size.
(N) Did he explain to you how they got them? How did you get to see them?
(D) Well, after they started to bring the stuff in—the second day I saw it.
(N) Let's backtrack a little. Did Geist work in that department before they brought the things in?
(D) He visited there. He'd talk to the older guys who worked there. He did sit down and take a hand occasionally or watch over my shoulder.

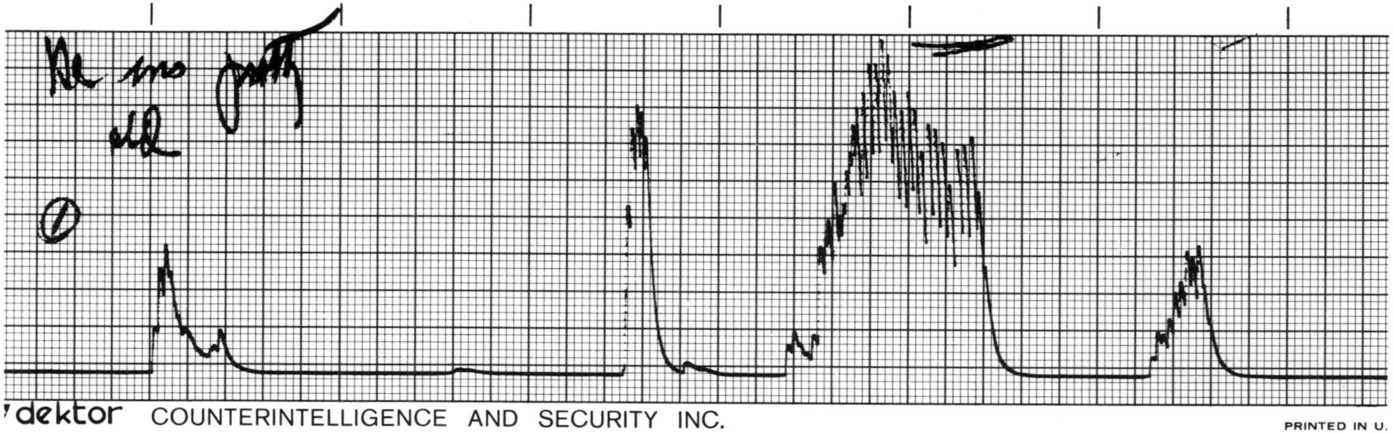

The *Psychological Stress Evaluator* and its boxwood-type patterns turned negative when examining Davis's statement that Robert Geist was "well, pretty old" (1). The dense needlework in the middle of the graph indicates severe tension and absence of microtremors which is typical when a subject is telling a lie.

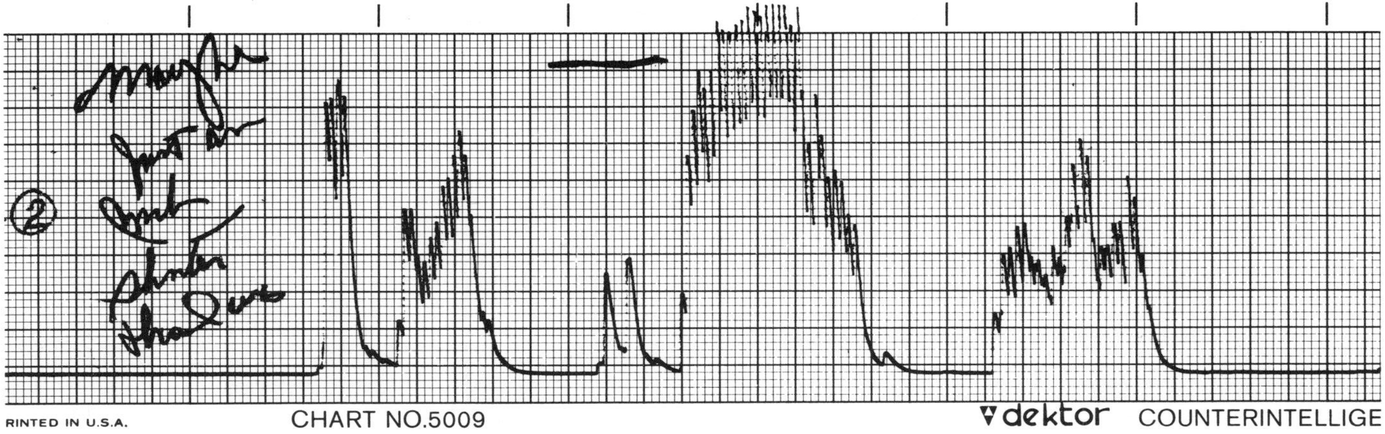

When Davis commented, "About an inch shorter than I was," referring to the elusive Dr. Geist, the same negative reaction showed up, again signifying an untruth (2).

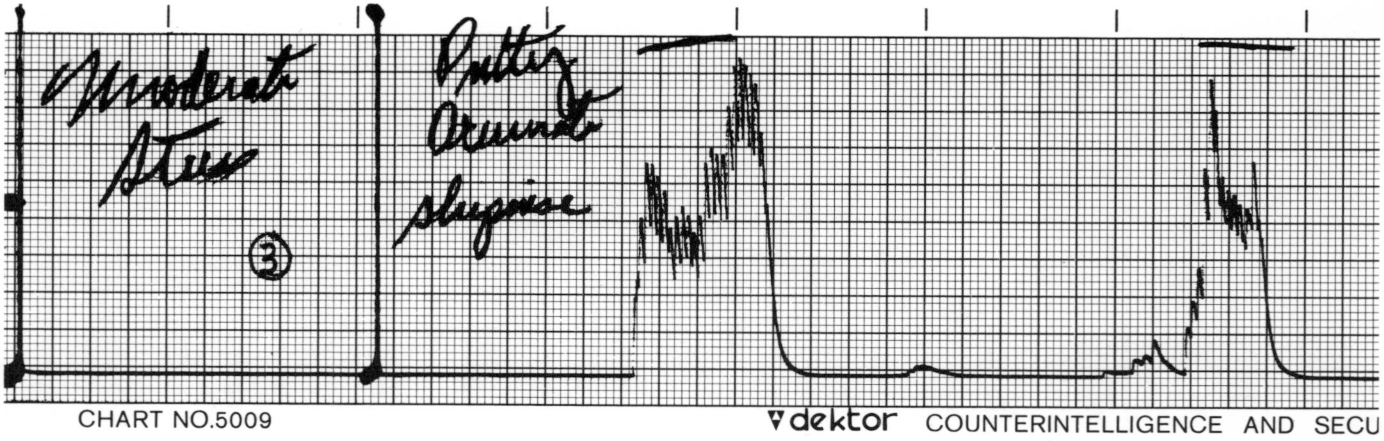

Commenting, "I'd say it's pretty accurate shipwise," referring to the drawing he had made which was to represent the photographed ark, he again showed a stress pattern, indicating mental conflict.

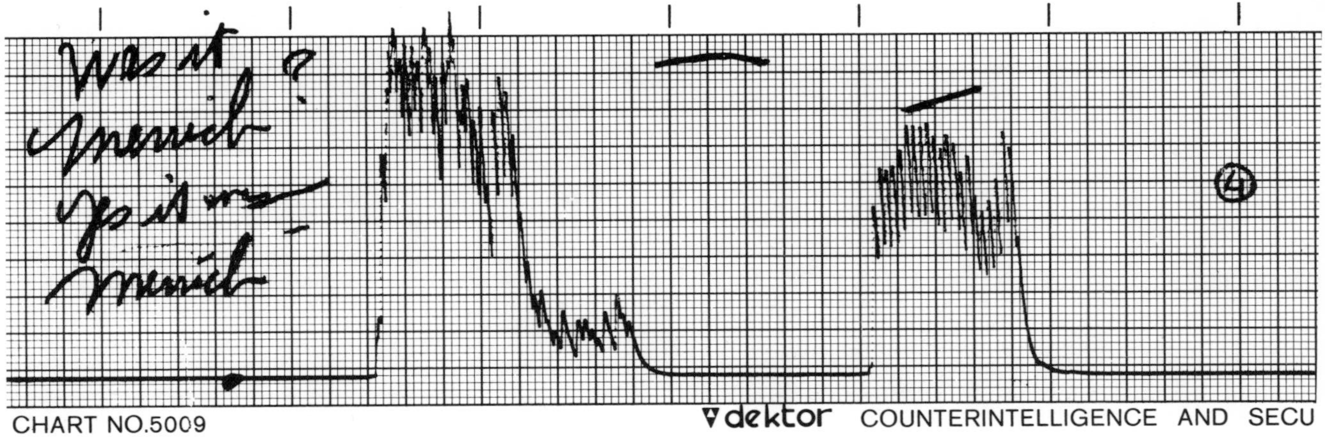

There was a discrepancy as to who had told Davis the artifact was the ark. He was emphatic about both Geist and Myrick as the one who told him. The PSE tested his answer. His answer, "Yes, it was Myrick," tested out untruthful. The reaction lacked microtremors.

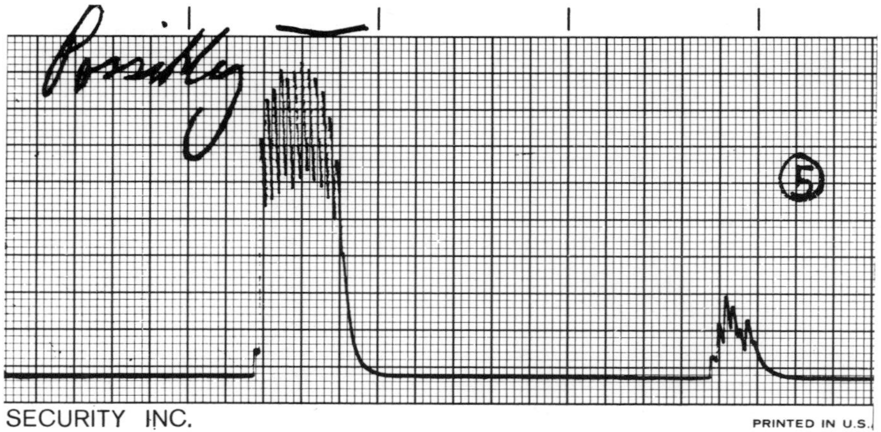

When Davis said Geist was convinced the ship was the ark because (referring to the sanitation set-up) "he said that's the only way it could *possibly* have worked," he created one of the clearest lie patterns yet. It was a tense statement which could not be taken any other way.

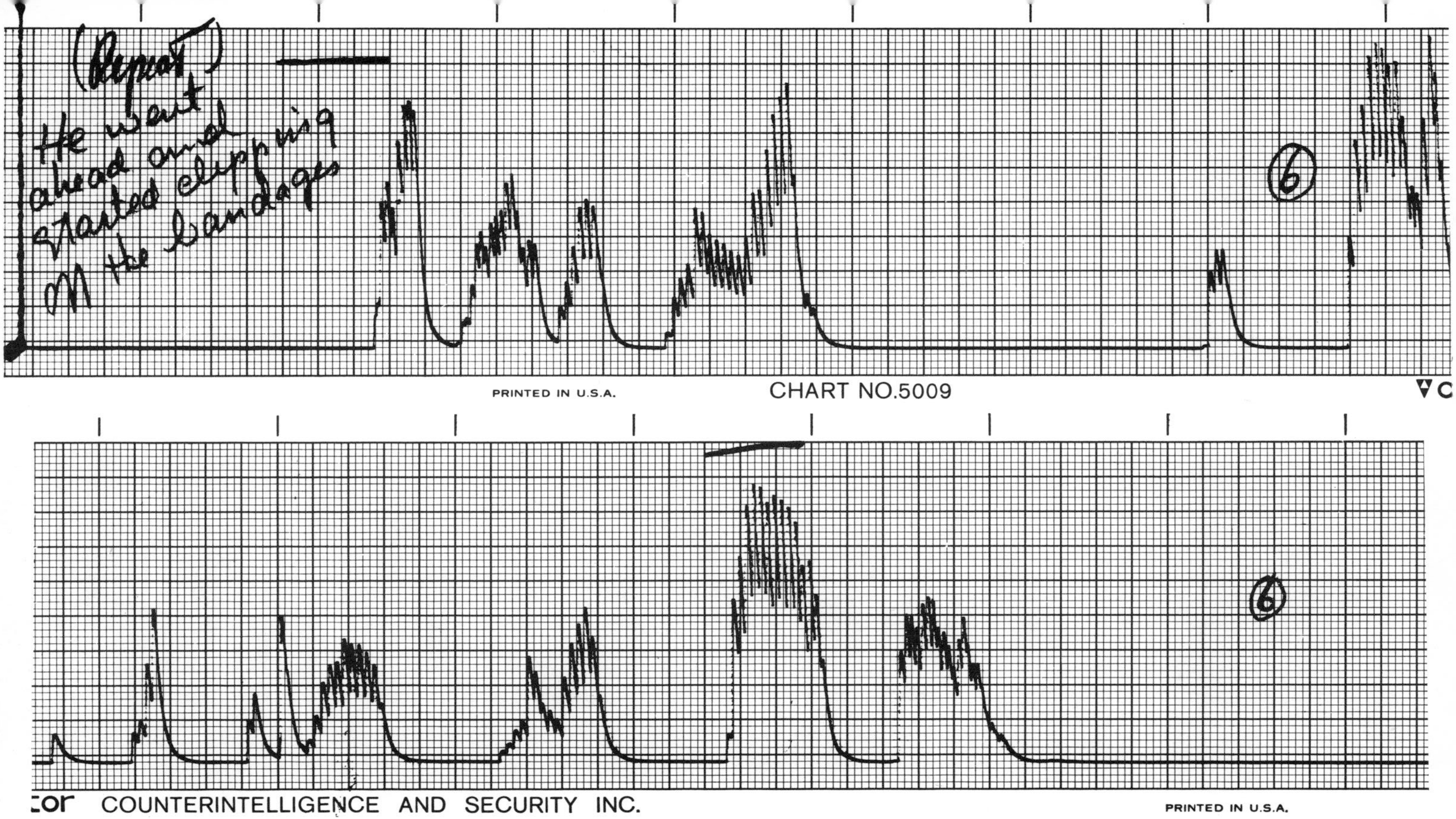

"He went ahead and started clipping off the bandages," Davis said, referring to Rice's actions with the body in the sarcophagus. The PSE indicated a repeated stress pattern on that answer, again denoting a deceptive answer.

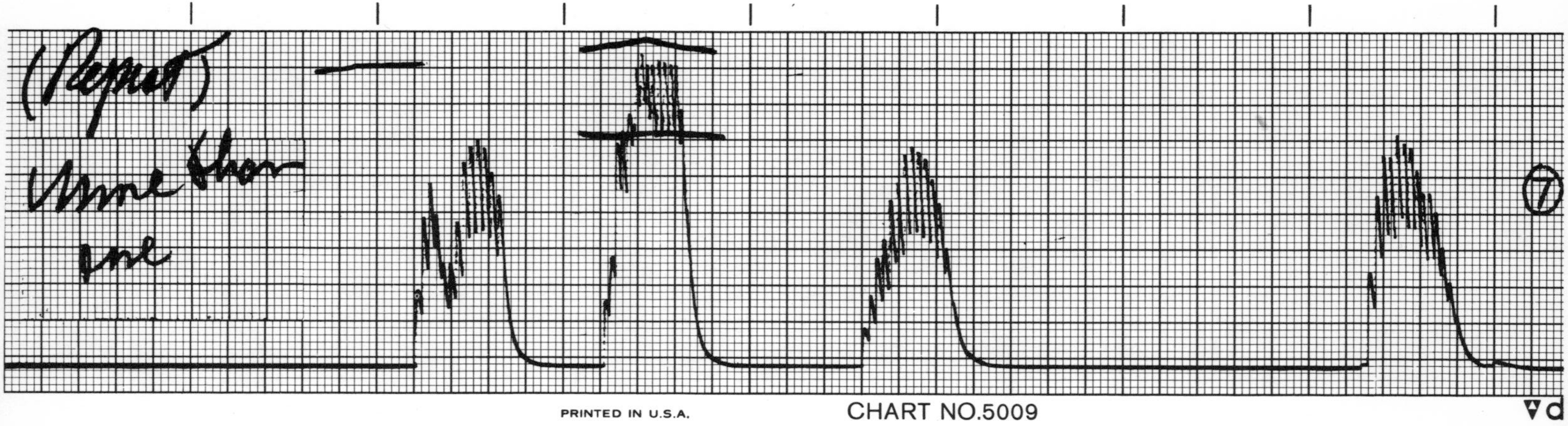

"They said 'these others,' so probably *more than one,*" commented Davis referring to the bodies that supposedly remained in the ark waiting for recovery. His answer created another clear pattern—classic boxwood patterns which denote a deceptive answer. There certainly were no more bodies hidden in whatever it was he had in mind.

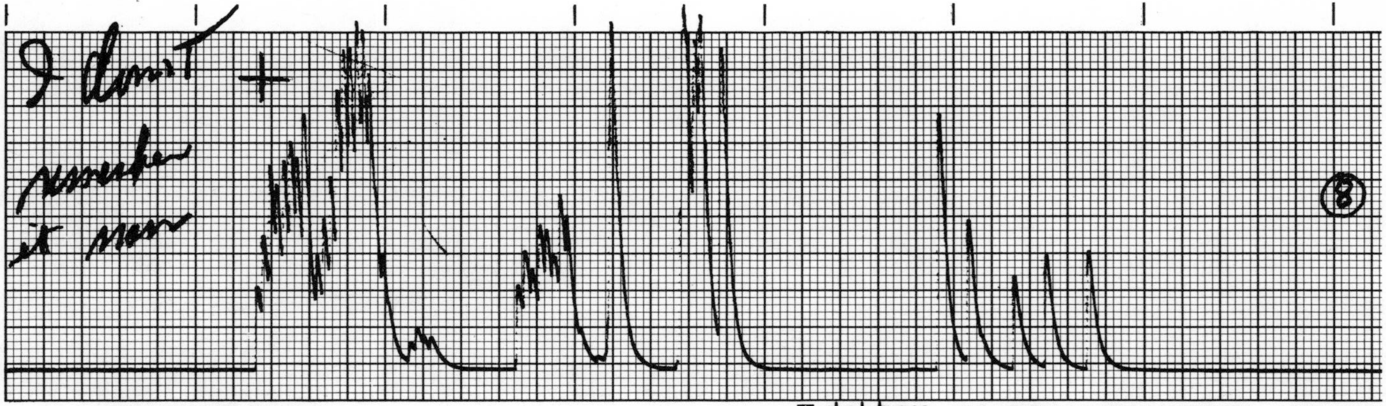

"I don't remember it now"—talking about the middle initial of the legendary Dr. Robert Geist—he made a true statement, for all the vocal overtones, the microtremors, were in place, indicating that the answer was supplied without presence of stress. Understandably he couldn't remember the middle initial, for Geist seems to have not existed at all.

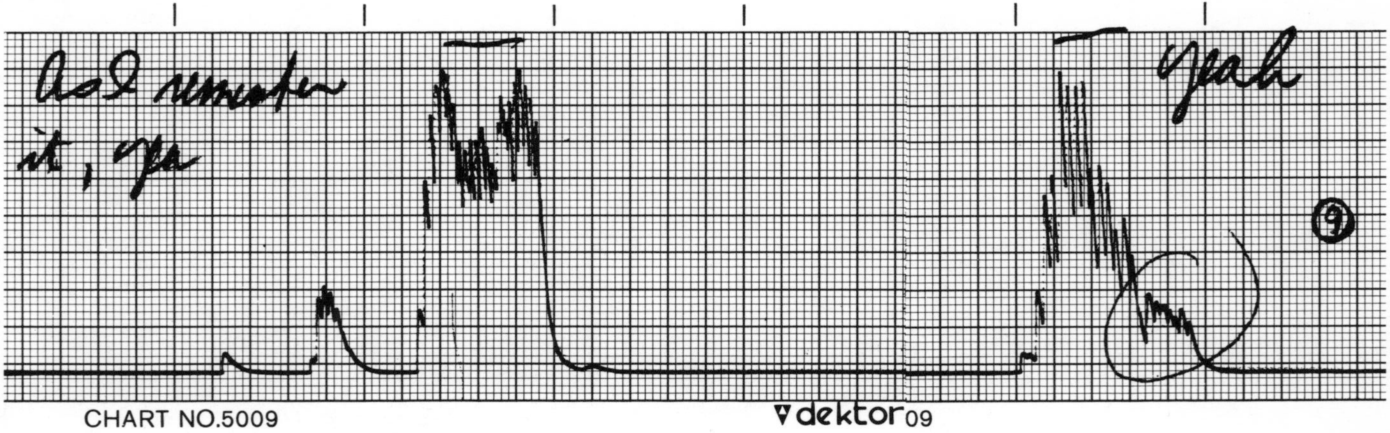

Davis's account of both the names of the National Geographic Society and the Smithsonian Institution appearing on the crates that were brought in, also was put to the Psychological Stress Evaluator. Answering to the question, "Both names were on these crates?" he replied, "As I remember it, yeah." The pattern traced by the PSE is conclusive. The statement was not true, and he could not have remembered it because he did not see it.

(N) What specifically did you do?
(D) Well, I was in a sort of training program. Volunteer help. They needed some extra help because they had a big backlog of fossils. Before the stuff came in, he'd come in a couple of times a day.
(N) Did you get the impression that he was well-known to the people [in the lab], or did he strictly come in as a part of the project and just happened to know a few people? Was he an "old-timer"? Did he really know his way around there?
(D) He seemed to know. He knew Myrick pretty well.
(N) How do you spell Myrick?
(D) I don't know. Just Al Myrick.
(N) When the crates were brought in, how big were they? How were they marked? What were they made of?
(D) They were brought in through the receiving department down from us. Regular wooden crates. Most of them regular-size crates like an expedition would have. One—perhaps two—were big. They measured three by four by two, or three by five by two feet. As for any kinds of marks, there were purple stamps on them. Not stamps, but rubber stamps.
(N) How were they marked? Any names or addresses on them? Smithsonian or Geographic or anything?
(D) I think that some of them were marked "Property of National Geographic/Smithsonian" and a date, you know.
(N) Both names were on these crates?
(D) Yes, as I remember.
(N) It is a long time ago. Do you remember how many boxes came in?
(D) About six of them and the box.
(N) What kind of a box was that?
(D) An oblong box maybe seven feet long, four feet wide.
(N) Could it have been longer?
(D) Possibly yes. Could have been wider, but was about seven.
(N) How about its height?

(D) Maybe four feet.
(N) Wooden box?
(D) No, carved out of alabaster.
(N) Did it come in a wooden box, and did they take the crate off?
(D) No. I didn't see a crate. There were some ropes holding it to a skid when I saw it.
(N) Any inscriptions?
(D) No, just a sarcophagus.
(N) Lid?
(D) At the end. A sliding lid. Was like this, set in the end in two slots. It had two holes in the top.
(N) Talking about the box—you said a while ago that you went upstairs where Rice worked and looked in through the door.
(D) Yes. I looked into the door. We stopped by and he said, "Well, how do you like this, man?" And I said, "Real nice!"
(N) The body was seven feet long?
(D) Shorter. It was human size.
(N) You said it was not wrapped? How did you describe it?
(D) It had been put into a linen bag, so they got the sarcophagus in and they'd taken it [the body] out the day before, as I understand; and he [Rice] went ahead and started clipping off the outside bandages, and they really came down on him.
(N) Did he tell you who came down on him? Anyone? Any names?
(D) He said the director—his boss. And they took the body down the hall and put it in a room—security.
(N) Security guard?
(D) Yes, with a security guard, and they locked the door.
(N) You said you don't recall Geist having much to do with that department upstairs with the body. Does that mean that he was mostly with the wood downstairs?
(D) Yes. Now it's possible that Geist was upstairs all the time, but since I was downstairs I wouldn't know.

(N) How about the identification of the wood? You mentioned something about the crystals. Do you recall what you told me about that?

(D) Well, Geist had the wood out. He was going over it with a magnifying glass, a jeweler's lens, and he was saying, "Notice the crystallization in the pores here. Typical of such and such a period." And like he'd say, "Notice how these holes were burned out with a hot drill!" It was held together with wooden pegs. He thought that was pretty interesting. He said that's how he figured they would have done it, you know.

(N) Do you recall him saying that this was really Noah's ark?

(D) No—uh—it was Myrick. Myrick said, "Hey, they've got Noah's ark there on the platform." That's why I went out there.

(N) How did you describe the pieces of wood they got out of the crates?

(D) Well, there were different fragments. There were beams and planks. He had one section of the hull. At least you know the wood was curved. It was real heavy blacky wood, you know, very roughly cut and everything, with dried caulking in the seams. Just put together you know with long wooden pegs.

(N) We were talking about this sketch you made. You mentioned that the burned-out hole in the deck was large enough so that three people could stand in the hole.

(D) Yes.

(N) Did you get the impression from them that the sarcophagus you were talking about came up through that hole? Or had it been brought out through the side?

(D) It was taken up through the hole.

(N) Did you get the impression that there were still more bodies in there?

(D) Yes. Dr. Geist and Myrick, they were looking at the pictures and said, "Now, the next time we're going to have to break in here in order to get the rest of them out because this won't work up through the shaft, you know."

(N) Did they give you any indication as to how many might still be in there?
(D) No.
(N) But at least two more.
(D) They said "these others," so probably more than one.
(N) This could mean that the one they took was probably the smallest.
(D) It's possible. That hole wasn't very big. It must have been hard getting it up through there. I didn't see any indication on the pictures of any block and tackle though, or lifting mechanism.
(N) Did anyone give you an indication of the height of the ship?
(D) Well, it's under ice. There are a few beams on the surface.
(N) You mean it is not exposed? It is under ice and only a part of it is sticking out?
(D) Yes. Up here at the bow, where it is all busted, that is above ground. That's the way it looked to me.
(N) Do you have any idea how they took these photographs?
(D) Balloons suspended over the wreck. On the photographs you could see like the wires, kind of automatic camera.
(N) Do you have anything else on this that might be interesting? Something I haven't asked, but which came into your mind while we were talking?
(D) Just a few details on the ship itself. One of the rooms—one picture taken through the ice looked like a barn room. Like in the picture the floors were slightly slanted like this, and there was this draining trough from the center. Now they described it to me as being a long hall like this with a lot of rooms on the side with small apertures in there for air, and you know, feeding troughs, set up for animals.
(N) So they were convinced that this thing had been set up for animals?
(D) Definitely. Geist—the reason he finally accepted it was the way the sanitation had been set up. He said that's the only way it could possibly have worked. It must have had a centralized

gathering place to get rid of it, if it [the ark] sailed around as long as it [the Bible] said it did.

(N) Did they give you any indication as to whom they thought might be in the box?

(D) Gene told me they thought it was Noah.

(N) Was this his opinion, or was it based on something they had told him?

(D) It was based on something they had told him, otherwise he could not have come up with it. I seem to remember one time coming back when he said like, "Hey, you know who they've really got in that box? Noah, man! Yes, they found him in the wreck, preserved, and a tablet with him."

(N) Did you guys discuss this on the way home, or what?

(D) Yes, but we finally stopped. They got pretty bad there. You know at first it was a happy place, but after this it wasn't much fun. Everybody was tight lipped; nobody had any time. They were going to conferences. I didn't see Myrick very much. He was always gone. Seldom saw Geist.

(N) Were you still there when the project was finished?

(D) No, I left. We were getting transferred. Actually the deal was I wanted to go into the Army education. I quit school in the fourth grade, and I figured I needed some more education, so I joined the program the Army was giving. In order to do that I had to leave.

The interview was finished, and for a few moments we relaxed, chatting about everything but the ark.

Then I popped a few last questions.

"Are you willing to take a lie-detector test?"

Startled, Davis looked at me. "Sure—no reason not to."

"How about sodium pentathol—truth serum?"

"If it's done right, yes." He shrugged his shoulders. "You know, it happened so long ago that some things I remember; some little things, and maybe some of it is wrong remembering. But eighty percent of what I've told you is just about true. Whether I saw the boxes while going to lunch or just going to see them, I don't know. I saw them, and that's what counts."

"We intend to solve it this year." I watched Daryl carefully, anxious for his reaction.

"I'd like to see it. I'd like to be in on it when you do! It does exist, and it did happen," he said, defending himself. "And if the Government itself is covering it up, then the people will be mad; if the museum is covering it up, then the people and the Government will be mad at them. Somebody is going to get locked up!"

"At least," I countered, "somebody is going to get in trouble!"

This was one point on which I could readily agree, for the last interview had finally brought things to a head. It was not the additional details he had squeezed into the third taping that sounded the warning; it was his considerably improved memory that alarmed me. Very casually, as if he had merely overlooked them before, he introduced some very pertinent fragments of information, which was to me an unexpected development and an indication that we were certainly heading for a climactic finish.

Once back in the familiar atmosphere of my library, it didn't take much effort to draw up a comparison chart covering the three separate interviews, crossing off the similarities and concentrating on finding a solution for the obvious inconsistencies that hung there, staring me in the face.

They were simply too pronounced to be ignored.

Faulty memory could account for his hesitation as to the exact time when his employment with the Smithsonian had commenced. He had worked there; that was an established fact. Thus the precise date was really inconsequential. However, from that date on, his story changed with the passing of time. Whereas he did not see the "body" in the casket in his first two interviews (February, 1972), in the last one (December, 1973) he had seen the mummy and even described the shroud in which it was wrapped. By now Rice's role had also changed. In the first version, Eugene Rice had merely cleaned the coffin with acetone. In the second interview he dusted off the body; while on the third tape he was caught clipping off the bandages. Robert Geist was in charge of vertebrate paleontology in the first interview, was the director in the second, and finally a visiting scientist in the third. In both the first and second interviews Davis claimed he had no idea of the size of the ship; yet at the same time he drew a sketch of the artifact indicating its length to be approximately 140 feet. This is far too short to be Noah's ark, since it would mean that the ark's size was based on a cubit of 5.6 inches —a cubit measurement unheard of in history. Puzzling also was the discrepancy in regard to the person who told him the artifact was the ark. "It was Geist," he said in the second interview; yet in the third he named Myrick.

There were just too many inconsistencies for us to contend with.

I grabbed the phone and called Daryl.

"Are you available this coming Sunday for a lie-detector test?" It was a suggestion unprecedented in the annals of ark research. As a rule, anyone coming up with a believable tale is accepted as a bonafide eyewitness, and his story is recorded as such.

Reluctantly Daryl agreed to the request, scheduling the test for the following Sunday morning.

It was a day to remember, for while Jim Wilson, the lie-detector expert who had joined me in Albuquerque, and I were on the way to his home from the airport, our storyteller left his house, not to return until after our departure late that night.

Was he afraid to take the test?

I did not want to base any conclusions on his hasty retreat alone, but it was obvious that he felt his credibility would not be affected by avoiding us.

Too bad he had never heard of the PSE.

For several months I had been considering introducing a new scientific instrument, the psychological stress evaluator, into the research; and, with Davis backing out of the agreed lie-detector test, this was an ideal time.

Invented by Allan D. Bell, Jr., president of Dector Counter-intelligence and Security, Inc., of Springfield, Virginia, the machine, similar to a conventional polygraph, shows the stress moments a person encounters when consciously attempting to give a deceptive answer. The main difference, however, is that whereas with the polygraph the subject must be hooked up to the machine in order to record his change in heart rate, blood pressure, blood oxygen content, and respiration, the PSE needs only the subject's voice—and then not even in the presence of the machine.

"When a person is relaxed and responding honestly to questions," Bell says, "inaudible frequencies in the voice register clearly on the machine. But when a person is under stress, as he is when he is lying, these frequencies drop out. Those listening can't tell, but the machine can." It is the machine's capacity to detect and reproduce these tremors—apparently caused by the freely undulating throat muscles of a relaxed speaker—that gives the PSE it's awesome powers. The throat muscles of a person under stress are so tense that they produce practically no microtremors.

Tested on the TV program To Tell the Truth, it scored an accuracy of 94.7 percent in determining who the truth tellers really were.

As yet, nobody claims the machine is infallible, but an indication of its reliability is that its results have already been accepted in court cases in various states such as Maryland and California.

Davis's total lack of cooperation to keep his appointment with the lie detector propelled the investigation into the direction of this new scientific development.

Early the following morning I was joined in my room at the Albuquerque Airport Marina Hotel by a local PSE operator. It took only ten minutes for Mike Susloski to hook up the equipment and another twenty to feed it a series of selected questions. We began by ten in the morning, and by noon it was all over. Ended were months of research, hectic trips to the Middle East, relentless combing of newspaper files and incessant concern over the identification of the body in the Smithsonian. The moment the tape began rolling through the machine, scribbling its verdict in indelible ink, the stress points in the story told of the innocence of the Smithsonian. Robert Geist was not old; he was not even shorter than Davis. He simply didn't exist. Neither did the body in the sarcophagus. And Rice? The markings recorded a moderate stress pattern on that question, indicating here too a possible untruth. One question after another revealed stress in various degrees, creating box-wood type patterns of tension we had not expected.

At 12:20 p.m. a mere twenty minutes before my plane was to leave, Mike summarized his findings.

"I would say," he stated authoritatively, "based on the looks of the excerpts we have taken from your tape and transferred onto mine, that there are stress patterns existing, and I would say that his answers are untruthful—overall untruthful!"

It was still difficult to surrender, and another attempt was made to persuade Davis to submit to a lie-detector test, if only to eliminate all doubt. A time was set—the next Sunday—but although the meeting was held, no test was given.

"He flatly refused," polygraph expert Wilson reported after three fruitless hours of negotiating. "He is only willing provided you will never see the results."

It's always a relief to reach the end of a trail, but somehow this was an empty victory. The only conclusion that could be crystallized was that another hoax had been uncovered, this time one of major proportions. If a discovery of this magnitude had indeed been made by the Smithsonian and the National Geographic, a cover-up might conceivably have been effected. But it seems most improbable that any such attempt would ever be made by any reputable scientist. Looking back over the "evidence" presented by Davis since his emergence from obscurity in February, 1972, it now becomes obvious that his information was gleaned from his eventual target; for the same organizations which so triumphantly published the *New Eden* account as "basically true," who regarded the *Rosseya* story of Colonel Koor as accurate and highly reliable, and who supported Archdeacon Nouri's discovery tale, as well as Navarra's discovery, now became the recipients of their own propaganda, but now in a slightly altered form.

There was, for example, a striking similarity between Davis's ship sketch "drawn from memory" and the Turkish aerial photograph of the 1960 expedition. The stone or wooden structures adjacent to the ship as mentioned by Davis were also previously reported in 1960. In addition, the first modern rumors pertaining to possible bodies in the ark were discussed during the same time period, while details concerning it were published even long before that—in 1684—in Gregory's *Notes and Observations.* His statement that the ship was deeply embedded in an ice flow might well have been borrowed from the *Rosseya* account, and the description of darkened pieces of ancient timber partially crystallized were first mentioned by Navarra in 1955 and have been making newspaper copy ever since.

Actually, Daryl Davis had nothing new to say, but all these highlights combined certainly formed the basis for a fascinating story.

And some people fell for it!

* * *

Where does this leave the search for the ark?

The answer depends upon who is doing the talking, for few

other subjects are as controversial and debatable as this one. Because of this continuing interest in Bible vindication, tens of thousands of dollars have been poured into research with the aim of locating the ark. Thus far the funds freely given have produced only untold frustrations within the many expeditions made.

Unfortunately, some of the projects have been conducted under circumstances which leave unanswered questions about motives and methods. A "sacred project desecrated by unprincipled hands"—this is the characterization made by a member of one expedition. And the same could be said of other groups that have operated in Turkey in the past quarter of a century.

Too often a yearning for personal glory seems to have been the motivating factor in all too many of the searchers for the ark. It is understandable that if a Supernatural Power has preserved the ark for more than 4,000 years under the adverse conditions prevailing on Mount Ararat, He certainly did not have in mind the glorification of the discoverer.

Let's consider for a moment the attitude of the Turkish government. If the situation should be reversed, how would we react?

Would our voice remain silent if during a similar time period, over forty expeditions from Russia would arrive in this country and claim to be searching for an archaeological artifact somewhere in the Rocky Mountains, and would continue to do so season after season without attaining their objective? Wouldn't we become suspicious when we realized that some of these groups operated without archaeologists or linguists, without experienced cartographers or other relevant disciplines represented? Wouldn't our uneasiness increase on discovering that many of these teams were supplied with army equipment and that their permits were usually granted through "gifts" to politicians, direct political pressure, or private contacts with the highest ranking military men in the country? And how would our government react to newspaper articles in which these groups were accused of being engaged in covert intelligence operations?

Incredible as it sounds, this is what has been happening in Turkey. No real effort has ever been made to cooperate with the Turkish scientific community aside from the few casual contacts. Confusion breeds division, and division breeds inactivity. Could these be the reasons that Noah's ark has not been found resting peacefully on some mountain ledge?

Is there another way?

There must be!

Since 1949 most Turks have been excluded from knowing the work and background of the various expeditions. But the project is legitimate. History and research show that there was and possibly still is a ship conforming to the proportions of the Biblical ark somewhere on the mountain. For a project of this stature, there is no need for scaling Agri Dagi under false pretenses. Even the few Turks who are cognizant of the inside details of the research realize the importance that discovery of the ark would mean to religion and to the tourist trade. Far-ranging plans already include luxury motels at the foot of the mountain, airlifts and helicopter pads, aerial trams to the ark site, and a huge plastic dome to cover and protect the artifact, topped by Disneyland-type amusement parks.

Frustration runs through every group. I believe that several constructive steps should be taken to help ensure ultimate success:

Unification of the various ark groups into one cooperative fund-raising unit should be a prerequisite to all further actions. The appointment of a Turkish-American group of businessmen to oversee the allocation of resources should be a close second. Coupled to this, a carefully planned public-relations campaign should be executed in Turkey, exhibiting displays of documents, photographs, and other visual aids explaining the search and its historical background. This would eradicate the quarter of a century of misconceptions that have entangled the search for the ark. Finally, of course, an all-Turkish team, together with a few selected Western researchers, should comb Agri Dagi and all other possible sites.

For there was an ark. It "rested in the seventh month, on the seventeenth day of the month, upon the mountains of Ararat." So speaks the voice of history.